Local Food and Community Development

Food has become an essential component in community development practice. Whether in reference to building a local or regional food system or addressing food insecurity, food has become a focus in community development approaches in many localities. Farmers markets, community gardens, farm-to-school programs, and other food-centered initiatives have been used to foster community development processes across a spectrum of desired outcomes. The surging interest in food for fostering community development draws attention to numerous applications, ranging from grassroots efforts to formal programs sponsored by the public or nonprofit sectors. These efforts are often in conjunction with local private businesses, helping create micro-businesses and supporting the small farm movement. Some regions are even considering economic development strategies of "food clusters" to promote speciality food businesses and supporting programs.

This volume explores the relationships between food and community, and the various approaches for development through a selection of chapters illustrating a wide range of applications.

This book is a compilation of articles published in the journal *Community Development*.

Gary Paul Green is a Professor in the Department of Community & Environmental Sociology at the University of Wisconsin-Madison and a community development specialist at the University of Wisconsin-Extension. His teaching and research interests are primarily in the areas of community and economic development.

Rhonda G. Phillips, Ph.D., AICP, CEcD is Associate Dean for Barrett, The Honors College and a Professor at Arizona State University's School of Community Resources & Development. Her research and service outreach includes assessing community well-being, and quality-of-life outcomes. She teaches courses on local food systems and community development.

Community Development – Current Issues Series
Series Editor: Rhonda G. Phillips

The Community Development Society (CDS) in conjunction with Routledge/Taylor & Francis is pleased to present this series of volumes on current issues in community development. The series is designed to present books organized around special topics or themes, promoting exploration of timely and relevant issues impacting both community development practice and research. Building on a rich history of over 40 years of publishing the journal, *Community Development,* the series will provide reprints of special issues and collections from the journal. Each volume is updated with the editor's introductory chapter, bringing together current applications around the topical theme.

Founded in 1970, the Community Development Society is a professional association serving both researchers and practitioners. CDS actively promotes the continued advancement of the practice and knowledge base of community development. For additional information about CDS, visit www.comm-dev.org

Tourism, Planning, and Community Development
Edited by Rhonda G. Phillips

Community Development Approaches to Improving Public Health
Edited by Robert Ogilvie

Community Economic Development
Edited by Rhonda Phillips and Terry L. Besser

Community Leadership Development
Theory, Research and Application
Edited by Mark A. Brennan

Cooperatives and Community Development
Edited by Rhonda Phillips and Vanna Gonzales

Local Food and Community Development
Edited by Gary Paul Green and Rhonda Phillips

Developing Sustainable Agriculture and Community
Edited by Jeffrey Jordan and Lionel J. Beaulieu

Local Food and Community Development

Edited by
Gary Paul Green and Rhonda G. Phillips

LONDON AND NEW YORK

First published 2013
by Routledge
2 Park Square, Milton Park, Abingdon, Oxon, OX14 4RN

Simultaneously published in the USA and Canada
by Routledge
711 Third Avenue, New York, NY 10017

Routledge is an imprint of the Taylor & Francis Group, an informa business

© 2013 Community Development Society

This book is a reproduction of a collection of articles from *Community Development*. The Publisher requests to those authors who may be citing this book to state, also, the bibliographical details of the special issue on which the book was based.

All rights reserved. No part of this book may be reprinted or reproduced or utilised in any form or by any electronic, mechanical, or other means, now known or hereafter invented, including photocopying and recording, or in any information storage or retrieval system, without permission in writing from the publishers.

Trademark notice: Product or corporate names may be trademarks or registered trademarks, and are used only for identification and explanation without intent to infringe.

British Library Cataloguing in Publication Data
A catalogue record for this book is available from the British Library

ISBN13: 978-0-415-63414-4

Typeset in Times New Roman
by Taylor & Francis Books

Publisher's Note
The publisher would like to make readers aware that the chapters in this book may be referred to as articles as they are identical to the articles published in the special issue. The publisher accepts responsibility for any inconsistencies that may have arisen in the course of preparing this volume for print.

Printed and bound in the United States of America by Publishers Graphics, LLC on sustainably sourced paper.

Contents

Citation Information	vii
1. Introduction *Gary Paul Green and Rhonda Phillips*	1
2. Everyday Meanings of "Local Food": Views from Home and Field *Marcia Ostrom*	8
3. Rethinking local business clusters: the case of food clusters for promoting community development *Davis F. Taylor and Chad R. Miller*	22
4. The influence of community capital toward a community's capacity to respond to food insecurity *Jessica Crowe and Justin Smith*	35
5. Localizing Linkages for Food and Tourism: Culinary Tourism as a Community Development Strategy *Gary Paul Green and Michael L. Dougherty*	53
6. Investing in the social fabric of rural and urban communities: a comparative study of two Alabama farmers' markets *Abel Duarte Alonso and Martin A. O'Neill*	64
7. "Growing Wellness": The Possibility of Promoting Collective Wellness through Community Garden Education Programs *Michelle L. D'Abundo and Andrea M. Carden*	82
Index	95

Citation Information

The following chapters were originally published in various issues of *Community Development*. When citing this material, please use the original page numbering for each article, as follows:

Chapter 2
Everyday meanings of "local food": views from home and field
Marcia Ostrom
Community Development, volume 37, issue 1 (2006) pp. 65-78

Chapter 3
Rethinking local business clusters: the case of food clusters for promoting community development
Davis F. Taylor and Chad R. Miller
Community Development, volume 41, issue 1 (2010) pp. 108-120

Chapter 4
The influence of community capital toward a community's capacity to respond to food insecurity
Jessica Crowe and Justin Smith
Community Development, volume 43, issue 2 (2012) pp. 169-186

Chapter 5
Localizing Linkages for Food and Tourism: Culinary Tourism as a Community Development Strategy
Gary Paul Green and Michael L. Dougherty
Community Development, volume. 39, issue 3 (2008) pp. 148-158

Chapter 6
Investing in the social fabric of rural and urban communities: a comparative study of two Alabama farmers' markets
Abel Duarte Alonso, Martin A. O'Neill
Community Development, volume 42, issue 3 (2011) pp. 392-409

Chapter 7
"Growing Wellness": The Possibility of Promoting Collective Wellness through Community Garden Education Programs
Michelle L. D'Abundo, Andrea M. Carden
Community Development, volume 39, issue 4 (2008) pp. 83-94

Introduction

Gary Paul Green and Rhonda Phillips

There has been a growing criticism of the global food system (Pollan, 2006). Concerns raised by critics are numerous, including the impacts of the structure of agricultural production on the environment, health and nutrition, food security, and rural community well-being. Large-scale agriculture relies heavily on chemical inputs, such as fertilizer, pesticides, herbicides, and growth hormones. These chemicals have the potential of contaminating the water supply and endangering the health of farm workers and consumers. Our food system contributes to the high rates of obesity due to the high fat and sugar content in processed foods. Increased concentration and centralization of the food system in the hands of a few corporations may increase the cost of food for consumers, and also depresses commodity prices farmers receive. Many analysts believe that centralizing the food production system and placing control in just a few corporations increases the risk of disease and contamination in our food system as well. Finally, there continues to be fear that an industrialized farming system leads to the destruction of our rural communities on all fronts, including social and moral aspects (Berry, 2009).

The local food movement offers new opportunities to support small- and medium-size farms, reduce the environmental footprint of agriculture, and promote good nutrition (Allen, 2004). Regional producers, especially small farms, can bypass the agribusiness sector by selling products directly to consumers (Kloppenburg, Hendrickson & Stevenson, 1996). Given the dominance of large agri-food firms, some see the local foods movement as particularly supportive of small farms and of rural areas (although the rise of urban agriculture is conveying benefits to those areas as well). Local foods are often organically grown, creating fewer potential risks to farm workers and consumers. Guthman (2004) warns, however, that it is not appropriate to equate local foods with organic. Organic agriculture has been incorporated into large-scale agriculture in some instances. Overall, however, the local food movement seeks to fulfill the "triple bottom line" by creating jobs, improving the environment, and enhancing social justice.

The local food movement is driven largely by consumers. Consumers are demanding higher quality products, and willing to pay higher prices for these agricultural products. In addition, there is greater worry over the "food miles" associated with the global food system because of the impact transporting food long distances has on carbon emissions. Given the concerns with peak oil, a food system that is based on global trade raises important questions about its sustainability.

Locavores are defined as people who eat primarily food grown or raised in their region. The definition of "local" may vary, but most locavores limit themselves to products from a 100–200 mile radius. Although consumers are increasingly concerned with the environmental and health aspects of their food, there is an important social dimension to all of the local food systems that are discussed in the following chapters. Residents are attracted to local food institutions because of the opportunities for social interaction and the potential of helping local business owners. There are economic benefits to promoting local foods, but the social elements are often the primary motivations of consumers (and often for businesses).

The focus of this volume is on the impacts of local food systems on community development. The articles selected focus on some of the different social dimensions that result from promoting local foods. There is a persistent theme in the literature that emphasizes the important contributions local food systems make to community interaction, civic participation, and leadership (Lyson, 2004). These are often unintended consequences of a movement that focuses primarily on environmental and economic considerations. In addition, these chapters demonstrate the potential and value of local development strategies that identify and build on local assets (Green & Haines, 2011).

Connecting to community development

Food is central to individual and community well-being and represents a nexus for exploring community development (Phillips, 2012). Some context is needed as a background to the discussion of the relationships between local food systems and community development. There are myriad ways that community development is defined, across a variety of disciplines. We offer the following definition:

> Community development is both a process: developing or increasing the ability to act collectively; and an outcome: taking collective action and the result of that action for improvement in a community in any or all realms: physical, environmental, cultural, social, political, economic, etc. (Phillips and Pittman, 2009, p. 6).

Although cognizant of the skills of individuals, it is also about the social dimension, with social capacity or capital as a major factor facilitating community development and capacity building as an exercise in creating or increasing the stock of capital (Pittman et al., 2009, p. 81). It is this focus of community development on building capacity that holds much relevance for local food systems. Simply put, social capital or capacity is the extent to which members of a community can work together effectively to develop and sustain strong relationships; solve problems and make group decisions; and collaborate effectively to plan, set goals, and get things done. Building social capacity then in turn leads to accomplishing outcomes, and this can be quite powerful in the community development realm. Because of the collaborative nature of many local food systems activities, building social capacity may be a natural outcome. For example, food hubs and farmers' markets are collective in nature and rely on relationships to function effectively and sustainably. It seems that there is an inherent inclination towards community development within these activities.

The local food movement provides a natural bridge to community development, especially when considering additional community factors such as accessibility, inclusiveness, equity, and other dimensions of community development that enable more sustainable and just processes and outcomes (Christensen & Phillips, 2012). Further, local foods systems are compatible with many of the ideas of sustainability. For example, food production, processing, distribution, and consumption are all integrated into dimensions of a place, including economic, environmental, and social aspects (Berman, 2011). It is this dimension of place or "sense of place" that ties in directly with local foods—more often, both residents and visitors are seeking to source their foods and eating experiences locally.

To accomplish desired outcomes, it will require continued capacity building in local food systems. Community development has a strong role to play, in helping foster and develop community capacity to support local producers, as well as to encourage educational efforts on the value of local foods sourcing. Efforts aimed at strengthening systems will help in turn bolster the positions of local growers, processors and venues.

Local food systems and efforts can realize benefit from explicit linkages to values-based commitments inherent in both social economy and sustainable community development approaches (Connelly, Markey & Roseland, 2011). It is vital to pay attention to values of a local food system, lest, "the localization of consumption and production risks being limited to the fetishization of local food for the most well resourced consumers, based on principles that correspond more to weak sustainability and weak social economy approaches" (Connelly, Markey & Roseland, 2011, p. 314). If there are no connections to desirable outcomes or changes within communities, then it is not really representative of a movement or as an agent for positive change.

What are some of the values of a local foods system in relation to community development? It is part of the "supply chain" of a community and there are values associated with each of the links. This chain can be described as including: 1) the processes of growing, distribution, processing, consumption, waste management—all impacting the built, natural, and social environments; 2) preservation of cultural dimensions, including traditions associated with food; 3) impacts on local and regional economic well-being, helping stem loss of small and mid-sized working farms; and 4) impacts on local economies via local purchasing, keeping wealth in the area. In each of these areas, the relation to community development can be seen, especially as related to the sustainability aspects of economy, environment, and equity (social and cultural dimensions).

Varieties of local food systems

As we see in this volume, the local food movement has taken a wide variety of forms (Hinrichs, 2000). Many consumers are now familiar with the growing number of farmers' markets throughout the country. These programs focus on providing a direct link between agricultural producers and consumers. In most cases, the products in the markets are grown or processed by the stallholder. Farmers' markets tend to be decentralized in many cities and improve access to fresh vegetables to many neighborhoods. Farmers' markets offer residents with an opportunity to interact with others in their community, as well as generate income for local farmers and retailers.

Farm-to-school programs have proliferated in recent years. It is estimated that there are more than 2,000 farm-to-school programs serving more than 8,000 schools. These programs provide opportunities for regional producers to supply school systems with food for snacks and lunches. In many cases, farmers participate in educational programs to teach children about nutrition and healthy food options. The concept of the farm-to-school program has been promoted in colleges and universities, as well as other institutional settings. One of the advantages of these programs is that students are provided an opportunity to taste new foods they may not have tried before and gain a better understanding of the source of their food.

Community gardens are also considered an important piece of the local food movement. They provide opportunities for families to grow their own food and educate children about nutrition and the environment. Many schools are now adding community gardens as part of their educational programs. Urban gardens also have grown as a tool to promote food security among the poor. In some cases, gardens provide more than a source of food and social activity, they are used as the basis for rehabilitative work. For example, some organizations use gardens as training programs for at-risk youth or recently released prisoners.

Community support agriculture (CSA) is another popular strategy in many regions for promoting local foods. Most CSA farms are small, but they tend to be quite profitable because they have high net returns per acre. Consumers purchase shares in a farmer's crop each year and they receive a portion of that crop over the growing season. This arrangement reduces some of the risk to growers, while providing consumers with fresh, locally grown produce.

Finally, many communities are beginning to link local foods with tourism. There is a growing interest in regional cuisines, which can support local producers, restaurants, and retail establishments that promote local products. Culinary tourism often includes wine tours, cooking lessons, restaurants and retail establishments featuring local foods. Agri-tourism provides venues for tourists to visit farms and food production facilities; many of these have become quite popular such as Vermont's Cabot cheese making facilities owned and operated by a cooperative of farmers.

These examples are just a few of the innovative local food strategies that have been initiated over the past few decades. In many cases, small farmers combine strategies so they can reduce their risk and diversify their interests. Nonprofit organizations are applying strategies too, for a variety of purposes to help foster social and economic development goals, to name a few. All of these efforts, whether private, public, or nonprofit in nature can help foster a sense of place and community development outcomes.

Obstacles

There are some common obstacles that these different institutional arrangements tend to face. One of the most common problems is the difficulty in matching between the supply of and demand for food. Large institutions, such as schools and hospitals, need a large, steady supply of food which may make it difficult to source locally. This is why many institutions turn to food service companies because they can aggregate their supply enough to meet this demand. It becomes difficult for individual farmers to satisfy the demand for local produce. Cooperatives and other social organizations can help farmers work collectively to market their products locally.

Another obstacle is the processing and health/safety issues of local food. Many institutions require some processing of food, but local farmers may not have access to facilities that will provide them with these resources. School systems, for example, may require carrots to be processed because they do not have the equipment or facilities to process the food themselves. Many localities have built community kitchens or with existing food processors to address this issue. Similarly, if farmers process their food locally, it will require investments in processing facilities to meet the health and safety standards. The cost of establishing new facilities can be prohibitive for most small and medium size farms.

Finally, the local food movement has often been criticized for serving the interests of wealthy consumers because it is often more expensive than food purchased through the global food system. Part of the cost differential may be due to the fact that local foods are often organically grown, which is often more expensive. Some of the local food arrangements discussed in this volume attempt to deal with this criticism. More and more farmers' markets are willing to take vouchers from the Supplemental Nutrition Assistance Program (SNAP), often referred to as food stamps, in order to be more accessible to the poor. In Madison, Wisconsin the Madison Area Community Supported Agriculture Coalition has been working with the Community Action Coalition to find ways of making local food more affordable through subsidies. Some farmers' markets in the Phoenix metropolitan area have begun offering discounts to SNAP customers with the intent of increasing their purchasing power.

Structure of this volume

In this edited volume, we have chosen several articles that focus on the impacts of local food systems on community development. The case studies reflect a wide variation across regions and types of local food systems in the United States. These cases focus on several economic and social benefits that may accrue from local food systems.

Based on surveys of producers and consumers in Washington, Marcia Ostrom (Chapter 2) focuses on the everyday meaning of local food. She finds a considerable amount of agreement of how local is defined among producers and consumers, largely geographic (either county or multi-county). For consumers, local food is often associated with ideas of freshness, but is also assumed to be helping farmers in the region. One of the difficulties farmers had in defining "local" was that they produce primarily for wholesale markets so localness was perhaps more abstract to this population.

Davis Taylor and Chad Miller (Chapter 3) focus on the potential of local food clusters in promoting economic development. The concept of an industrial cluster has become popularized in the economic development literature. It is based on the premise that firms within a region are tightly connected. Taylor and Miller compare two different food clusters: the Maine Local Produce cluster and the Mississippi Catfish cluster. The Maine cluster focuses on production for local consumers, while the Mississippi cluster is a more typical export industry serving consumers outside the community. The two clusters offer an interesting comparison of how food clusters can be organized to create jobs and generate income.

Jessica Crowe and Justin Smith (Chapter 4) examine the issue of food security in several states across the United States. Based on a large sample of surveys, they found that social and cultural capitals are strongly related to the capacity of communities to provide alternative sources of food in communities. This study documents the importance of community assets in building a sustainable supply of food.

In Chapter 5, Gary Green and Michael L. Dougherty examine the potential and limitations of culinary tourism as a community development strategy. Culinary tourism features regional cuisine as a way to promote tourism. They conduct a case study of the

Kingdom So Delicious program in Door County, Wisconsin. Retail establishments in the region relied heavily on local farmers for produce. They stated that their primary reason for local sourcing was to support the community. Two key constraints face farmers: low prices and logistics (supplying retail establishments enough produce when they need it). This case study suggested that institutionalizing the linkages between producers and retailers would help ease some of the difficulties in the system.

Farmers' markets are probably the most common form of local food system. In the last few decades, there has been a significant increase in the number of farmers' markets across the United States. Abel Alonso and Martin O'Neill (Chapter 6) look at the social dimensions of two farmers' markets in Alabama. Based on surveys conducted of visitors, they find that the motives for participation in these markets were primarily social. Visitors reported that they went to farmers' markets for social interaction and to support local farmers.

Michelle D'Abundo and Andrea Carden (Chapter 7) discuss how community gardens promoted several dimensions of wellness in a low-income North Carolina community. An important recommendation is that educational programs on community gardening should go beyond programs on nutrition and gardening, but include the relational wellness of residents as well.

Taken together, these chapters improve our understanding of how local food systems can contribute to community capacity building and development (McKibben, 2007). They suggest it is possible to restructure our economy so as to build more sustainable and equitable communities by emphasizing social and environmental goals along with profits (Shuman, 1998). It is within these contexts that the value of local food systems can be realized in the context of community development.

References

Allen, Patricia. (2004). *Together at the Table: Sustainability and Sustenance in the American Agrifood System*. University Park, PA: Pennsylvania State University Press.

Berman, E. (2011). Creating a community food system: The Intervale center. *Journal of Agricultural & Food Information*, 12, 3–11. doi:10.1080/10496505.2011.539527.

Berry, W. (2009). *Bringing it to the Table: On Farming and Food*. Berkeley, CA: Counterpoint.

Christensen, Bradley, & Phillips, Rhonda. (2012). Local food systems and community economic development through the lens of theory. Unpublished paper.

Connelly, Sean, Markey, Sean, & Roseland, Mark. (2011). Bridging sustainability and the social economy: Achieving community transformation through local food initiatives. *Critical Social Policy*, 31, 308–324.

Green, Gary Paul, & Haines, Anna. (2011). *Asset Building and Community Development*, 3rd Edition. Thousand Oaks, CA: Sage Publications.

Guthman, Julie. (2004). *Agrarian Dreams: The Paradox of Organic Agriculture in California*. Berkeley: University of California Press.

Hinrichs, Claire. (2000). Embeddedness and local food systems: Notes on two types of direct agricultural markets. *Journal of Rural Studies*, 16, 132–143.

Kloppenburg, Jack, Hendrickson, John, & Stevenson, G.W. (1996). Coming into the foodshed. *Agriculture and Human Values*, 13, 33–42.

Lyson, Thomas A. (2004). *Civic Agriculture: Reconnecting Farm, Food, and Community*. Medford, MA: Tufts.

McKibben, Bill. (2007). *Deep Economy: The Wealth of Communities and the Durable Future*. New York: Henry Holt and Company.

Phillips, Rhonda. (2012). Food cooperatives as community-level self-help and development. *International Journal of Self-Help and Self-Care*, forthcoming.

Phillips, Rhonda, & Pittman, Robert (Eds.). (2009). *An Introduction to Community Development.* New York, NY: Routledge.

Pittman, Robert, Pittman, Evan, Phillips, Rhonda, & Cangelosi, Joe. (2009). The community and economic development chain: validating links between processes and outcomes. *Community Development, 40*, 80–93.

Pollan, Michael. (2006). *Omnivore's Dilemma*. London: Penguin Books.

Shuman, Michael H. (1998). *Going Local: Creating Self-Reliant Communities in a Global Age.* New York: Free Press.

Everyday Meanings of "Local Food": Views from Home and Field

Marcia Ostrom

A "buy local" approach to food sourcing appears to provide an increasingly salient mobilizing framework for city, county, and state level governments; non-profits; and funding agencies as a response to problems in the agri-food system. One rather constant source of tension, however, has been a failure to develop shared meanings about what constitutes "local food." This paper critically examines the multiple ways that "local" is constructed in physical, relational, and symbolic space within the specific context of Washington State. In hopes of extending the debate beyond scholars and activists, we sought the perspectives of a broad sample of Washington citizens using farmer and consumer surveys. Open-ended questions were asked about the meaning of "local food," as well as structured questions about the values and practical considerations associated with food production and marketing. Although a number of obstacles to using "local food" as a mobilizing construct to address systemic agricultural problems became evident, a surprising amount of agreement about the meaning of the concept was also uncovered.

As encapsulated in the rallying call to "think globally, eat locally," efforts to privilege and promote "local" food sourcing are gathering momentum in many parts of the United States. A recent proliferation of media stories,[1] campaigns by non-profits, and Web-based organizing efforts[2] have sought to heighten awareness of local food buying options and the benefits of local purchasing among the public and government policy makers. In many of these written accounts and promotional campaigns, reconnecting local consumers with local producers or "localization" is positioned as one of the most promising antidotes to an ailing American agricultural system that is increasingly being squeezed by low-cost overseas production, high input costs, intensifying environmental regulation, and a consolidating food manufacturing and distribution sector. Recent books such as *Going Local* (Shuman, 1998), *Coming Home to Eat* (Nabhan, 2002), *Eat Here* (Halweil, 2004), and *the Case Against the Global Economy: and for a Turn Toward the Local* (Mander & Goldsmith, 1996), along with a growing body of academic work investigating food system "localization" and place-based marketing strategies (Barham, 2003; Hendrickson & Heffernan, 2002; Hinrichs, 2000, 2003; Kloppenburg et al., 1996; Lacy, 2000; O'Hara & Stagl 2001; Pretty & Lang 2005), build a compelling case for the economic, environmental, and socio-cultural benefits of establishing shorter, regionally-based, food chains and linkages. Shuman (1998) explains that in contrast to conventional economic development paradigms that focus on attracting outside investors with mega projects, strengthening community-based food and farm businesses offers a locally owned and controlled development process that can retain profits and conserve the natural resource base.

It could be argued that "local food" has become the unifying theme of a social movement to challenge and reshape the modern agri-food system, with "local" coming to signify all that is believed to be the antithesis of a globally organized system where food travels great distances, is controlled by behemoth, transnational corporations, and is wrought with environmental, social, and nutritional hazards. A "local food" paradigm, in contrast, emphasizes food quality and freshness, a personal connection to small and family-scale farms, environmental protection, community self-reliance, and the economic multiplier effects of making local purchases. Growing concern with the cost and instability of fossil fuel supplies is further inspiring interest in locally-based food production and distribution chains from the standpoint of energy efficiency (Kunstler, 2005).

A "buy local" approach appears to be providing an increasingly salient mobilizing framework for city, county, and state governments; non-profits; and private funding agencies. For example, Woodbury County, Iowa, recently passed a resolution titled, "the Local Food Purchase Policy," that mandates the purchase of locally grown food by county institutions. At least ten state governments are now reported to have passed legislation urging or requiring state institutions to increase local food purchasing (Flint, 2004). The federal government is also subsidizing numerous grassroots efforts to develop "buy local" campaigns, regional labeling programs, "farm locater" databases, and farm directories through its agricultural granting agencies. Prospective food buyers can now search for farmer vendors in any state or zip code in the country.[3]

As the stakes in the marketplace grow, what is becoming increasingly contested is the meaning and scope of "local." A search of the literature and Websites focused on this topic reveals that very few writers have attempted to construct a definition for "local food," and these definitions are inconsistent. In his popular book, Nabhan (2002) sets out a spatial definition of a 200-mile radius. Other authors propose units of analysis ranging from 12 miles (Pretty & Lang, 2005), to 30 miles (Flint, 2004), to a day's round-trip drive (Devine, 2004). One Website campaign provides criteria for ranking "degrees" of local with categories ranging from 1 to 3,000 miles.[4] The local purchasing resolution passed by Woodbury County defines local as "that food which is grown and processed within 100 miles of Sioux City, Iowa."[5] Beyond its physical scale, other aspects of "local food" as a mobilizing construct are also contentious. Hinrichs (2003) fears that a focus on "local" can be used to obscure socially or environmentally unsustainable production practices or reinforce a parochial bias against outsiders or "others," a tendency she alternately refers to as "defensive localism" or "food patriotism." Allen et al. (2003: 74) observe that a preoccupation with creating particularized solutions to food and farming problems at the local level may divert attention away from the need to confront social justice issues effectively in the agri-food system at a broader scale, positing that "oppositional stances cannot be successful when they are only local: they require the power of a broader social movement to prevail." Thus, Hinrichs (2003: 295) points out that, "as both matter and symbol…'local food' can hold multi-faceted and sometimes contradictory meanings." While food system localization has proven to be a powerful mobilizing concept, she warns that it can also be a "perilous trap" (302).

Snippets from a recent flurry of electronic messages on a list serve used by farmers and community food activists in the Northwest provide a glimpse of the passion and ambiguities associated with this concept. A week-long exchange was set off when one writer expressed disappointment that food from over 100 miles away was labeled as "local" in his farmers' market. Another contributor sympathized, declaring that even under "100 miles is not local." "Local," offered another, "means a place I can walk or bike to." A farmer who earned her living in the Seattle farmers' markets countered that she considered herself "very local to that city" and felt personally connected to her many devoted customers there, despite living over 100 miles away. Another farmer's viewpoint was that "if a farmer can load the truck in the morning, make the delivery, and get back home the same day," the food should be considered local. Contributors variously contended that "local" should be constructed in accordance with climate zones, natural features, bioregions, or the energy required for transportation. As the conversation wore on, the questions grew more complex. "What if food was raised two miles away, but stored or processed hundreds of miles away?" "Should the distance associated with 'local' vary depending on the crop, the season, the fossil fuels consumed, or one's location?" "What about the origin of the inputs used to produce the food—how many producers have equipment or vehicles that were locally made or use seed that was locally grown?"

Ultimately, it was proposed that the term was so multi-layered and contradictory as to be meaningless. "I think the idea of 'defining' local makes no sense whatsoever." "When you really consider the full chain of production," wrote another, "it is nearly impossible to make absolute claims of 'local.'" Yet, as the e-mail volley wound down, the conversation returned to the farmers' market question and the very real need for better communication between producers and consumers in the marketplace as they seek to build new kinds of relationships based on commonly held values and interests. It was finally agreed that since the term was being so widely used it should be defined.

Despite creative evolutions in thinking about food in relation to such concepts as "foodsheds" (Kloppenburg et al., 1996), "agroecosystems" (Conway, 1985; Flora, 2001) "home" (Nabhan, 2002), or "place" (Kemmis, 1991; Jackson, 1993), as illustrated by the example above, little conceptual progress has been made in developing a shared concept of "local." A rich literature, however, has evolved around the concept of "community." Community development theorists have built a strong case for conceiving of "community" as both a physical and a social or interactive space (Wilkinson, 1991; Liepins, 2000). Increasingly, attention has been accorded to the notion of communities as dynamic social networks formed on the basis of shared interests, values, and identities that are continuously being recreated and reinforced through interactive discourse and practice (Flora, 2001; Liepins, 2000). When viewed from a community development framework, rather than "defensive localism," identification and a sense of attachment to a "locality," be it material or symbolic, can be viewed as a way of building social networks and generating the social capital necessary to catalyze community action around improving markets and government policies (Flora, 2001).

The intent of this paper is to further the conceptual development of the term "local" as it is applied to food systems. Theories of community will be drawn on to explore the ways that "local" is socially constructed in physical, relational, and discursive space within the specific context of Washington State. In order to extend the debate beyond scholars and activists, surveys were utilized to analyze and compare the perspectives of a broad cross-section of Washington consumers and farmers. We expected that the meanings assigned to this term might vary for different types of stakeholders. For example, producers, who pragmatically need to earn a living from markets wherever they might happen to be, may have different perceptions than consumers do with less at stake. We also thought that views might vary according to proximity to the major urban markets in the state, socio-economic status, the regional availability of different foods, agronomic zones, and various cultural and regional identities.

As part of two large-scale, agricultural marketing and policy surveys, one of consumers and one of farmers in Washington, we asked an open-ended question about the meaning of "local." We have not seen any reports of similar random sample, large-scale surveys with farmers or consumers asking them to describe "local" in their own words. While it cannot be argued that such surveys are the definitive way to answer a question of such a complex and contested nature, it is nonetheless the most cost-effective way of hearing from the broadest possible number of people.

STUDY METHODS

Two separate data sets were analyzed for this study (*for methods see also* Ostrom & Jussaume, 2006). The producer data was collected from a large-scale, mail survey of Washington State farmers.[6] By special permission, we drew a sample from the state list of all Washington farm operators maintained by the National Agricultural Statistics Service (NASS). Ten percent of farm households in each county was sampled. In the spring of 2002, questionnaires were sent to 3,718 farm addresses. A series of follow-ups, including a post-card reminder and two additional survey mailings, were conducted with non-respondents using Dillman's (2000) Tailored Design Method. We received 1,201 completed surveys. Removing ineligibles and non-completed returns from the original sample left a completion rate of just over 49%.[7] This rate appears to be reasonable for a general farmer survey of this type when compared with similar surveys from other states.

Follow-up calls with non-respondents to discover response bias were impossible since we did not have access to the NASS phone numbers. A comparison of the farm characteristics of respondents with the Agricultural Census, however, indicated that our sample was fairly representative of the state in terms of the types of commodities produced, with 10% producing vegetables, 28% fresh fruits, 28% hay, and 35% cattle. We had slightly higher percentages of fruit and vegetable farmers than the state averages in the Census. We also probably had a slight overrepresentation of large farms.

A telephone survey was utilized to collect consumer data. Because of the huge expense entailed in surveying the whole state, we elected to focus intensively on four counties that we felt represented the state's diversity. These were the four target counties: 1) King County, a large urban county where Seattle is located; 2) Skagit County, a semi-rural county in western Washington with relatively small, diversified crop and livestock farms; 3) Chelan County, a rural, eastern county characterized by mid-sized tree-fruit orchards; and 4) Grant County, a very rural, eastern county characterized by highly industrialized, large-scale, irrigated, row cropping systems. The population for the survey included all telephone households located within the four counties. A random digit dialing approach was used to obtain the sample.

A random sample of 5,200 telephone numbers was selected, with 1,300 in each target county.[8] Calling took place between October and December 2002. Interviewers asked for the person in the household, 18 years of age or older, who was most involved with food buying. A maximum of 12 call attempts was made to each number and 950 total respondents (at least 230 per county) agreed to participate in the survey. The overall response rate of 23% is currently considered standard for a telephone survey.

Open-ended questions about "local" were phrased slightly differently on the farmer and consumer surveys. Consumers were asked: "What does locally grown or produced food mean to you?" Farmers were asked: "What would you consider to be your local market?" A follow-up question to farmers inquired: "What changes would have to occur in order for you to sell more of what you grow in local markets?" The responses obtained from these open ended questions were transcribed, coded, and analyzed according to the open and axial coding system delineated by Strauss and Corbin (1990). Data were coded in relationship to the place where the respondent lived.

Consumers were also presented with a series of structured questions asking them to rate the importance of various purchasing values, including "locally grown," "grown in

Washington," "organic," and "helping local farmers." Finally, they were asked to rate their interest in purchasing particular products directly from local growers. Farmers were asked whether they agreed or disagreed with various statements about the desirability of having more local foods available in their county, the value of direct marketing in their county, the importance of a "Grown in Washington" label or a "buy local" campaign, and their opinions on various agricultural and marketing policies. They were asked what percentage of their products were sold to consumers in their county, in adjoining counties, in the state, in the country, and out of the country.

Pinning down the local

Similar to the multi-faceted debate surfacing around the meaning of "local" among activists and academics, respondents provided highly varied and often unique answers to our open-ended survey questions. Perhaps indicating fairly widespread interest in the topic among consumers, most did elect to describe what "locally grown" meant to them, with less than 5% declining to answer the question. Farmers, on the other hand, were more likely to skip this open-ended question, with over one-fourth leaving a blank when asked to describe their "local market." This may partially reflect a higher tendency to skip open-ended questions on mail surveys in comparison with phone surveys, but it probably also reflects the fact that a large proportion of Washington farmers do not feel they have any local markets for their products. Upon analyzing the characteristics of the farmers who skipped this question, a large number turned out to be producers who relied exclusively on wholesale markets.

When reviewing their responses, it initially appeared that farmers and consumers had interpreted the questions in such a multiplicity of ways that no meaningful patterns would emerge. Among farmer and consumer samples, there were contingents that identified the scope of "local" at scales ranging from the backyard garden to the neighborhood, town, county, state, country, or the globe. There were others who constructed the concept of local according to natural features such as valleys or river basins, inland waterways, the Pacific Coast, a Northwest bioregion, or by climate zones, such as maritime or arid. Other responses about distance were indeterminate, using phrases such as "nearby," "close," or "right here." Interestingly, while most consumers chose to define "local" in terms of a distance or a geographical scale, a significant subset associated it with the characteristics of the food such as "fresh" or "pesticide free" or simply "better." Another group associated it with the characteristics of the farmer or a relationship with a farmer, using adjectives such as small, independent, trustworthy, or known. Finally, some responses emphasized the socio-economic benefits of local purchasing for communities.

Many consumers did not see the various scales of "local" as static or discrete, indicating a fluid definition of "local" that varied depending upon the products and the climate zones where they were grown. Comments reflected the very diverse nature of Washington's agricultural zones. For example, one person stated that "local lettuce comes from the Skagit Valley, but local peaches would be from Washington State" or another described "local" as "the Wenatchee Valley for apples, the Yakima Valley or a 100-mile radius for other products." Thus, "local" appeared to radiate outward depending on the product and its regional availability.

On the farmers' side, a significant number interpreted their "local" market as the local sale barn (livestock), processor or packer (fruits and vegetables), or grain elevator, despite the fact that these "buyers" were actually wholesalers or brokers who would redistribute or resell their products to wide-ranging destinations. Other farmers who sold to these same outlets interpreted the question differently, either explaining that they did not actually have "local" markets or describing the redistribution of their products to in-state, domestic, or international buyers. Finally, rather than using spatial descriptors, some farmers described their local markets in terms of customer characteristics or typologies, such as urban or middle-class consumers, tourists, specific types of other farmers, or "acquaintances." Table 1 conceptualizes these primary types of responses to the open-ended questions and shows their frequencies. Most commonly, respondents constructed "local" using geopolitical boundaries, supplying the names of towns, counties, or states. Over a third of both consumer and farmer respondents conceived of a scale for "local" in such geopolitical terms.

Table 1. Contrasting Ways of Conceptualizing Local

	Farmers (n = 1,166)		Consumers (n = 950)	
Distance or Time	6.4%	(75)	26.6%	(253)
Geopolitical Boundary (city, county, state, country)	38.6%	(449)	35.1%	(333)
Natural Feature or Climate Zone	7.4%	(86)	9.2%	(87)
Type or Name of Market Outlet	13.4%	(156)	1.9%	(18)
Characteristics of the Product	NA		13.1%	(124)
Characteristics of the Farmer	NA		5.3%	(50)
Characteristics of the Customer	5%	(58)	NA	
Economic benefits of local Purchasing	NA		1.8%	(17)
Other	1.5%	(17)	2.6%	(25)
Skipped Question	27.8%	(325)	4.5%	(43)

Spatial constructions of scale

Of all the definitions that were provided for "local," three-fourths were either explicitly spatial or could be approximated in distance-related scales (for example, many people listed a driving time or a geographical place name). One way to discover clearer patterns was to examine the responses that could be related to a spatial category separately. Removing the non-spatial types of references (i.e., those that focused on food quality or type, economic impacts, the categories of farmers or buyers, and the non-responses) left 696 consumer responses and 634 farmer responses. This subgroup was then sorted into discrete, standardized categories of scale, such as neighborhood, town, county, state, etc. References to environmental features, driving times, and place names were coded based on the resident's address, and answers were placed in the single category with the best fit. For consistency, comments citing multiple distances were coded according to the most expansive scale indicated.

Table 2 shows the frequency with which different loose categories of distance were cited among farmer and consumers. For consumers, the most commonly cited geographical scale for "local" was "the county and bordering counties," with nearly a third stating that food grown within their county or a neighboring county was "local." The second most frequent definition of local was "county," with just under 24% stating that food grown in their county was "local." The third most frequently named category was "Washington State," with almost 21% of consumers saying that "locally grown" food was food grown in their state. Farmers had somewhat similar spatial concepts of "local" as consumers, with the top three categories named in the same order of frequency. Within the group of farmers that responded in spatial terms, the vicinity of "county and bordering counties" was also the most commonly cited reference point, with 32% defining such an area as their "local" market. Again, the second most commonly cited definition was the respondent's county, with just over 23% describing this geographical unit as their "local market." The third most commonly cited region was the state, with 18% seeing this as their "local market."

Table 2. Interpretations of Local: Cumulative Frequencies by Increasing Scale

	Farmer		Consumer	
	Percent	Cumulative Percent	Percent	Cumulative Percent
Home or Neighborhood	1%	**1%**	3%	**3%**
City or Town	10%	**11%**	18%	**21%**
County	23%	**34%**	24%	**45%**
County or Nearby County	32%	**66%**	30%	**75%**
State	18%	**84%**	22%	**97%**
Northwest	8%	**92%**	2%	**99%**
United States	6%	**98%**	1%	**100%**
The World	2%	**100%**	0%	**100%**

Noticeable differences emerged in the way that consumers and farmers perceived the scale of "local." Consumers were far more like to identify "local" as their backyard, neighborhood, community, or town, than were farmers. Perhaps this is because farmers tend to live in more sparsely populated areas outside of towns and neighborhoods. However, it might also be that farmers were inclined to take a more expansive view of their "local" market than consumers. For example, farmers were more likely to cite the entire Northwest as their geographical reference point and a significant number (41 or 6%) named the United States as their "local" market. Moreover, eleven farmers stated that they considered the "world" to be their local market. In contrast, only six consumers (1%) said that their idea of "locally grown" encompassed the entire country, and none felt that it extended outside of the U.S. borders.

Much of the discrepancy between consumer and farmer scales for "local" probably reflects the way the questions were asked. When farmers were asked to describe what they would consider their "local market," rather than indicating that they did not have "local markets" or skipping the question, many farmers did their best to follow instructions and simply answered the question by describing their existing markets. In Washington, most farmers rely primarily on wholesale markets. For the top four crops in the state (wheat, apples, dairy, and beef) local marketing options are virtually non-existent or very limited. A close review of the responses shows that nearly all of the farmers listing the United States as their "local market" were apple growers who market through packing houses for national and international distribution; producers of vegetables and fruits grown under contracts for large-scale processors, such as Simplot; and cattle producers. Those who listed international markets as "local" primarily raised wheat for export to the Pacific Rim. Another way to interpret the responses that identified U.S. markets as "local" is to realize that for these growers, "local" is relative. Among wheat and lentil producers for whom nearly all crops are exported, by comparison, anything used domestically could be considered "local." For example, when asked to describe "your local market," one wheat and legume farmer wrote:

> Anything that is for domestic consumption, i.e., Krusteaz uses soft white wheat, Centennial mills at Cheney will use Zak wheat. The Spokane Seed Company sells our split green peas to packagers, including Campbell's soup.

Thus, while at first it may appear contradictory that so many farmers listed national and international markets as "local," describing their markets in such expansive terms makes sense in the context of the crops they raise and the way the question was worded.

Overall, there appeared to be some areas of relative agreement when comparing and contrasting different perspectives on the scale of "local." Examining the cumulative frequencies of spatial references in progressively broader, nested levels of scale, as shown in Table 2, reveals some discernable patterns. The majority of both farmers and consumers see the limits of "local" as a neighboring county or nearer. While even more consumers than farmers drew this boundary, these perceptions did not vary significantly by the respondent's area of the state, proximity to the major urban markets, or by agricultural zone. By the state level, virtually all the consumers (97%) and the vast majority of the farmers (84%) have reached the outer limits to their concept of "local."

These results from our Washington Survey were similar to a random sample telephone survey of 500 citizens in the Northeast in which 16% defined local as an area smaller than a county, 22% as the county, 16% as an adjacent county, and 31% as the state. The majority (54%) felt that local implied an adjoining county or closer, and more than 85% felt that local implied their state or closer (Wilkins et al., 1996). While this survey is not directly comparable to ours since it was done in 1996, used different methods (i.e., the answer categories were provided rather than being open-ended and the percentages include the "other" category), and spanned multiple states, it does suggest some common conclusions. Just as in Washington, most of the people surveyed saw the limits of local as their county or a nearby county and very few people had a concept of local that extended beyond their state. In our Washington survey, the only significant group that defined "local" more broadly than the state borders were the farmers who raised crops such as apples and wheat for national and international export markets.

Qualitative and relational attributes of "local"

Analyzing the second subset of survey responses (those that did not contain explicit spatial or geographical markers) revealed that "local" was frequently framed in qualitative or relational terms. On the consumer surveys, over half of the comments without a spatial reference, instead, made an association with freshness or the superior quality of the food, using comparatives like: fresher, tastier, purer, healthier, and better. For example, one person wrote, "It would taste better because it is fresher, and it was picked when it was supposed to be" or "products are fresher because they are picked the day of purchase." Others observed that locally grown means "fresher, higher nutritional value, quality is better" and "it has fuller flavor and texture." A content analysis of all the consumer responses to the open-ended question taken together confirmed the strength of this free association of "freshness" with "local." The word "fresh" or one of its derivations showed up 228 times or on one-fourth of the total responses to the open-ended question. Concepts of freshness and quality were closely intertwined with other positive product attributes such as "pesticide or antibiotic free" and "natural."

A second, related theme running through many of the comments was an association of "local" with supporting or having a relationship with a specific, idealized type of farmer. This farmer was described alternately as: small, pesticide-free, kind towards animals, hard-working, trustworthy, honest, or independent. The following quotes illustrate this association of "locally grown" with particular types of farmers:

> Locally grown food means foods that are produced close to home with little to no chemicals, primarily by small producers, which perhaps means more humane conditions toward meat and poultry than some of the larger places.

> It is extremely important that the community supports eating food that is grown in the area. It's healthier and supports smaller farmers instead of agribusinesses.

It was very important that a "local" farmer would be a real person whom you would know and trust and have a personal connection with, someone whom you could see and talk to face-to-face. It was repeatedly stated that "locally grown" meant "food grown here from *somebody*" or food "grown in the area by *farmers*." Many people emphasized that they liked the idea of buying the food directly from the person who had grown it because "you would know what you're getting."

> The farmer knows exactly what has been planted, what has been put on the plants, what's been put on the land, selling fresh and organic products, and the farmers are involved.

> I would know the farmers and they would know me and I would trust them. They would be honest and wouldn't try to sell me inferior products.

Thus, knowing how the food was grown and who grew it were very important to many people, and they associated having access to this knowledge as a benefit of "locally grown" food. They also liked the idea that they, personally, were helping a farmer to succeed with their purchasing choices, making statements like, "It means we are supporting the farmer, and he can stay on his farm," or "It makes me feel good to buy from a local vendor."

Sentiments about supporting the farmers were tied up with a strong interest in supporting their community's economy in general. Statements such as, "If I buy it, I'm contributing to the local economy," were common. Another explained that buying locally grown food "keeps people in our area working—there's not a whole lot around here." Some respondents said that they bought as much locally as they could based on principle, whether food or other items, "to help the local person instead of going to the big company" or to "keep the money in our area." Some responses combined these various associations, but in virtually every case, the qualitative associations with "locally grown" were either positive attributes of the food, the farmers, or the economic impacts. While such statements were not spatial in a measurable way, they were spatial in that they described a particular scale for buying and selling food that would allow for personal, face-to-face relationships among farmers and consumers and a short time between harvest and sale.

On the farmer surveys, because of the phrasing of the question, as discussed previously, there were obvious reasons for not supplying a spatial definition of a "local market." Many producers did not feel they had a local market outlet for the kinds of crops they raised. Two of Washington's most commonly produced crops, apples and wheat, are primarily produced for export markets and almost exclusively sold through wholesalers. Beef, another top commodity in the state, faces substantial regulatory and infrastructural barriers to local and direct sales. Another large contingent of growers raises potatoes on contract for buyers like Simplot who in turn supply McDonalds and Wendy's chains. Thus, when asked what they would consider their "local market," many of these producers were understandably at a loss for an answer because they did not know who the end users of their products would be. They either explained that they had no local market, i.e., "We do not sell to local markets; we sell to packers that sell all over the United States and outside countries," or they detailed the characteristics of their sales venues. Of the respondents who did not provide a distance-related descriptor for their "local market," over three-fourths, instead, named a local wholesaler, packinghouse, or auction barn. Many of these respondents supplied the only information they knew about their product sales, i.e., "The packing shed handles the sales" or "In our co-op, I don't have a say in the sales--our marketing office sells for the best price no matter where that might be." A number of farmers who used wholesale markets did attempt to describe the location of the end-users of their products, making statements like "we have two market areas: foreign and domestic." It seems likely that farmers did not actually consider these to be "local markets," but they were just trying to figure out an acceptable way to answer the question.

A second group, mostly direct marketers, elected to detail the characteristics of their customers rather than the locations of their customers. Thus, customers were described variously as middle-income, well-heeled, health-conscious, urban, tourists, friends, or acquaintances. "My local market," wrote one farmer, consists of "upper-end consumers of organic or homegrown meat who are accustomed to shopping at specialty food stores." Another significant portion of this subset appeared to sell feed or livestock to other farmers, describing their "local markets" as cattle ranchers, hog producers, dairies, horse farms, etc. Of the whole farmer sample, only six respondents said outright that they did not know what it was or could not define their "local market," but such uncertainty was likely the cause of the huge number of skips on this question among farmers and the tendency to refer to wholesale buyers as a "local market."

Ranking "local" among other consumer values and interests

In a later section of the telephone survey, consumers were presented with structured questions about the importance of various food purchasing criteria. In keeping with several other surveys from around the country (Hartman, 2001; North Central Initiative, 2001; Leopold Center, 2004), we found that consumers were, above all else, concerned with the freshness, taste, and nutritional quality of their food (see Figure 1). The next most important value was "convenience." "Organic" appeared to be a relatively unimportant value. These top values varied little by household income category, except that "price" became increasingly important as income levels went down (Ostrom & Jussaume, 2006). While the open-ended survey comments about "locally grown" were almost uniformly positive, Figure 1 shows that, as a stand-alone concept, the importance of "locally grown" was ranked very low in comparison with other purchasing priorities. Interestingly, when the question was rephrased such that "local" was linked with "helping local *farmers*," its relative importance climbed dramatically from just under 34 percent of consumers ranking it as "very important" to over 70%. Similarly, having food that was grown in Washington, in and of itself, was "very important" to only 41% of consumers. However, again, if the question was phrased in a different way, such that it was linked with helping farmers the response changed. A separate question in the survey asked consumers whether they felt that having a "grown in Washington label" would help Washington farmers and 94% strongly agreed.

Again, when consumers were asked specifically about their interest in purchasing more fruits and vegetables directly from local *farmers*, interest was extremely high, with over 80% responding affirmatively. Looking back at the open-ended survey question asking people to define what "locally grown" meant to them, many consumers had equated "local" with a particular idealized type of farmer or their relationship to a farmer, making such associations as small, independent, pesticide-free, or trustworthy. Summarizing this data as a whole, the concept of "locally grown" as a stand-alone value is not nearly so strong

Figure 1. Percent Consumers Rating "Very Important"

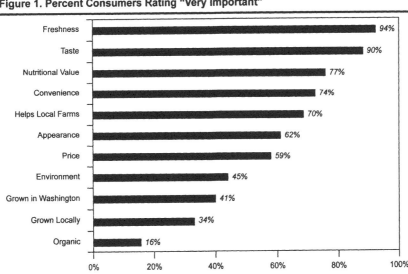

as the connotations or associations that come along with it. Consumers appear to be most interested in the concept of "local" when it is associated with desirable attributes of food quality, such as freshness, taste, nutrition, or safety (i.e., pesticide free) or associated with a local farmer. In turn, the concept of "local farmer" is constructed in very specific ways. Recent market research carried out by Iowa State University in the Midwest and key cities across the country shows similar results (Leopold Center, 2003, 2004). These researchers also concluded that conceptions of local foods were intrinsically tied up with perceptions about freshness, quality, and the ideal of the "family farm." They found that a label of "locally grown," when it was linked with "freshness" and "family farm" had more market appeal than all other product labels tested, including "organic."

Importance of local markets for Washington farmers

One survey question asked farmers to state the percentage of their crops sold to end consumers in their *county* or a *neighboring county*. Over half of all the respondents reported that they sold at least some of their crops to end consumers in their counties. Around 16% of the farmer sample said that they sold all of what they produce to in-county consumers. These numbers were probably inflated by farmers who sold livestock and feed directly to neighboring farmers. It is also likely that a certain number of farmers considered the local auction or packing plant to be an "end consumer" of their products. When asked specifically about their future plans to increase their use of direct marketing (in this case defined specifically as the "face-to-face" sales methods of farmers markets, roadside stands, Community Supported Agriculture, and "U-pick") over a quarter of all farmers and over half of vegetable farmers said they wanted to increase their use of these methods.

From the farmer's perspective, there are clearly significant obstacles to increasing local sales. A second open-ended question asked farmers what changes would need to occur before they could sell more foods locally. While these answers varied highly by the type of farm, most immediately obvious were statements about the regulatory and processing barriers to meat and value-added product sales, the limitations imposed by marketing contracts, and the oversupply of certain crops (especially apples) in relation to local market demand. Apple growers commented that "everyone would have to eat 15 more pounds of apples each year" or "reduce imports of competing fresh fruits" in order to create a local market for apples. In extremely rural areas, farmers made comments like, "We live in a sparsely populated county—what we can sell locally is limited," or "We would have to go beyond our county to reach people with money." One farmer in a sparsely populated, highly productive, agricultural county put it this way:

> Well, for starters, the locals would have to buy 7 million pounds of onions, 1 million pounds of peas, and 5.7 million pounds of sweet corn ... We are growing enough food for the nation and the world.

Another recurring sub-theme was the lack of inspected local processing facilities for meats, the lack of local milling and transportation options for specialty grain products, and the regulatory obstacles to creating and selling new kinds of value-added products on farms.

Farmers, as a whole, favored policies that encourage direct and local market development over international market development. For example, while approximately 77% of all farmers think that a "grown in Washington" labeling program would benefit Washington farmers, under a quarter believed that free trade agreements would help them. A majority of farmers believed that consumers in their counties should have access to more locally grown foods and that direct marketing could help keep farms viable in their counties. When asked for an opinion about the value of a "buy local" campaign, more than half agreed that this could increase the consumption of locally produced agricultural products. On all of the questions about local and direct marketing, however, there was a clear association between the type of crop grown on the farm and the farmer's support for these concepts. On practically every question, wheat growers (comprising most of the farmers in some eastern counties of the state) were far less likely to see the value of local or direct marketing or the importance of having more locally grown foods available. This belief is clearly related to the fact that, in these counties, virtually all crops are undifferentiated commodities grown for export markets. At present, it would be extremely rare for Washington wheat to be eaten by anyone in Washington State. Therefore, the idea of "local foods" carries very little relevance for this subset of producers at this time.

DISCUSSION AND IMPLICATIONS

While there were certainly many complex variations in the way the concept of "local" was constructed and interpreted by Washington residents, these survey results suggest that there may be more consensus about the relevance and meaning of this term than first suspected. Above all, our findings confirmed that most residents have positive associations and a strong common interest in the idea of local foods. Consistent with findings from studies of "communities," the various ways respondents constructed and delineated "local" were fluid and included physical, relational, and qualitative elements. Spatial perceptions of "local" among both farmers and consumers favored a fairly close distance of one's home county or neighboring counties, although consumer constructions of scale sometimes varied to incorporate the climatic zones within the state needed to obtain a variety of foods. Definitions of "local" generally stopped at the state borders, except for producers of particular commodities grown for national and international markets. Even farmers located far from the major urban markets were still inclined to describe "local" as their county or an adjacent county. Some farmers were clearly stymied in their efforts to conceive of local markets by the nature of the commodities they produced and the insufficient demand or infrastructure to market their products close to where they lived.

Consumer constructions of "local foods" were closely intertwined with positive perceptions about product freshness and quality and idealized images of "local" farmers. Purchasing local foods was seen as contributing to the success of desirable types of agriculture and a way of helping the community economy. These positive associations with "local" explain why marketing specialists from the grassroots to corporations have been so eager to capitalize on this term.

Clearly, at this point "local" is a message that works. These results would seem to argue for less paralyzing deliberation about whether "local" means: "within sight," 3 miles, 10 miles, 100 miles, or even within a state; and a greater pragmatic focus on overcoming the practical infrastructural and regulatory obstacles to local food system development. Conceiving of "local" using geopolitical boundaries such as counties or a state provides a definable space in which the environmental and social parameters of food systems can be assessed and democratic interests can be negotiated as illustrated by the effectiveness of county and state-level food policy councils (Hassanein, 2003). While the meaning of the term will certainly remain contested and a topic of healthy debate among scholars and activists, it already appears to hold some degree of shared meaning for the general public. It is important to consider whose interests are served by maintaining that the concept of "local food" is devoid of meaning or by defining "local" so narrowly that we have excluded most of the productive agricultural capacity of our rural areas. In so doing, we miss the opportunity to substantially change diets, energize and educate consumers, and effect the policy changes needed to engage the largest possible number of farmers in supplying regional dietary needs.

While more research is needed on the effectiveness of "buy local" campaigns, farm directories, and place-based labeling strategies, the evidence from our surveys suggests that most farmers and consumers will not find a failure to define "local" as an obstacle to participation. Instead, what seems to be needed is more transparent communication and interaction between farmers and consumers so that consumers can make informed purchasing decisions in the marketplace in keeping with their stated values. Consumers seem eager to know more about the actual farmers that grow their food, the growing practices they use, and the unique characteristics of the food. This desire is undoubtedly difficult at a scale as big as the state of Washington, especially since consumers place such a high value on convenience. In markets where face-to-face interaction is impractical, the Hartman (2001) researchers emphasize the importance of communicating with clear identifiers that describe the farmers, their unique growing practices and ecosystem, and their location. Communicating detailed information about the unique attributes of a particular farm and the food it produces provides an important way of connecting and building common ground among farmers and consumer interests and insuring that the term "local" cannot be appropriated by transnational corporations. Finally, it is through building common ground among consumers and farmers based on their identification with a "locality" and their common interests that the social capital needed to address the very real, practical barriers to local food distribution can be addressed.

NOTES

1 For examples see: Devine, 2004; Halweil, 2003; Flint, 2004; Mapes, 2004; Pierce, 2005; Raloff, 2003.

2 For Websites featuring local food buying campaigns, see: www.foodroutes.org; http://www.buylocalfood.com/about.html; www.eatlocal.net; http://www.ecotrust.org/foodfarms/; http://www.organicconsumers.org/btc.html; http://www.newfarm.org/features/0803/localfoodchall.shtml; and http://groups.yahoo.com/group/LocalFoodCafe Numerous other community Websites focus on local foods, many of them part of the "Buy Fresh, Buy Local" campaign started by the FoodRoutes Network (Website above).

3 The most extensive national farm locator Website currently is: http://www.localharvest.org/farms/M9006, however, countless numbers of regional groups throughout the country maintain their own databases and printed farm directories, guides, and maps, some of them established a decade or more ago.

4 See: http://groups.yahoo.com/group/LocalFoodCafe/ (downloaded on May 24, 2005).

5 For the full text of this policy, see: www.woodburyiowa.com/departments/economicdevelopment

6 The 2002 producer and consumer surveys were administered by M. Ostrom, R. Jussaume, and L. Jarosz with funding from the W. K. Kellogg Foundation, the WA Farming and the Environment Project, and the USDA-NRI.

7 The farmer survey had 46 refusals, and 1,047 ineligibles and returns. Ineligibles were defined as households that sold less than $1,000 in commodities in 2001, as well as those farm households that had moved, passed away, retired from farming, or received multiple surveys because they owned more than one agricultural property.

8 Of these 5,200 telephone numbers, 1,043 were determined to be business and/or non-working numbers and were removed from the sample. This made the corrected sample 4,157.

REFERENCES

Allen, P., FitzSimonns, M., Goodman, M., & Warner, K. (2003). Shifting Plates in the Agrifood Landscape: The Tectonics of Alternative Agrifood Initiatives in California. *Journal of Rural Studies* 19: 61-75.

Barham, E. (2002). Towards a theory of values-based labeling. *Agriculture and Human Values* 19 (4): 349-360

Barham, E. (2003). "Translating terroir: the global challenge of French AOC labeling." *Journal of Rural Studies* 19: 127–138.

Conway, G. R. (1985). Agroecosystem Analysis. *Agricultural Administration*, Vol. 20, pp 31-55.

Devine, D. (2004, December 4). Local Food Makes a Global Impact: The Case for Shopping Locally. *North Country Times*. San Diego, CA.

Dillman, D. A. (2000). Mail and Internet Surveys: The Tailored Design Method. New York: John Wiley.

Flint, A. (2004, August 15). Think Globally, Eat Locally: A new socially conscious food movement wants to reset the American table. *The Boston Globe.*

Flora, C. (2001). Shifting Agroecosystems and Communities In Cornelia Flora (Ed.), *Interactions between Agroecosystems and Rural Communities*. Boca Raton, FL: CRC Press. Pp. 5-13.

Halweil, B. (2004). *Eat Here: Reclaiming Homegrown Pleasures in a Global Supermarket.* Worldwatch Press. Order at: www.worldwatch.org ISBN: 0-393-32664-0. 237 pp.

Hartman Group (2001). *Food and the Environment Update, An Industry Series.* Report. Bellevue, Washington. Download at: http://www.hartman-group.com/products/reports.html

Hassanein, N. (2003). Practicing Food Democracy: A Pragmatic Politics of Transformation. *Journal of Rural Studies.* 19: 77-86.

Hendrickson, M., & Heffernan, W. (2002). Opening spaces through relocalization: Locating potential resistance in the weaknesses of the global food system. *Sociologia Ruralis* 42 (4): 347-369.

Hinrichs, C. (2000). Embeddedness and Local Food Systems: Notes on Two Types of Direct Agricultural Market. *Journal of Rural Studies* 16: 295-303.

Hinrichs, C. (2003). The practice and politics of food system localization. *Journal of Rural Studies* 19 (1): 33-45.

Jackson, W. (1993, October 23). *Becoming Native to This Place.* Thirteenth Annual E.F. Schumacher Lectures. Yale University, New Haven, Connecticut.

Kemmis, D. (1991). *Community and the Politics of Place.* Norman, OK: University of Oklahoma Press.

Kloppenburg, J., Jr., Hendrickson, J., & Stevenson, G. W. (1996). Coming in to the Foodshed. *Agriculture and Human Values* 13(3):1-10.

Kunstler, J. H. (2005). *The Long Emergency: Surviving the End of the Oil Age, Climate Change, and Other Converging Catastrophes of the Twenty-first Century.* Grove Atlantic, Inc.

Lacy, W. (2000). Empowering Communities through Public Work, Science, and Local Food Systems: Revisiting Democracies and Globalization. *Rural Sociology* 65 (1): 3-26.

Leopold Center (2003). *Ecolabel Value Assessment: Consumer and Food Business Perceptions of Local Foods.* Iowa State University. Download at: http://www.farmprofitability.org/local.htm

Leopold Center (2004). *Ecolabel Value Assessment Phase II: Consumer Perceptions of Local Foods.* Iowa State University. Download at: http://www.leopold.iastate.edu/pubs/staff/ecolabels2/ecolabels2.htm

Liepins, R. (2000). New energies for an old idea: Reworking approaches to 'community' in contemporary rural studies. *Journal of Rural Studies*, 16: 325-341.

Mander, J., & Goldsmith, E. (Eds.). (1996). *The Case against the Global Economy: and for a Turn Toward the Local.* San Francisco: Sierra Club Books.

Mapes, L. V. (2004, February 8). It's What's for Dinner: Piling our plates with good intentions. *Seattle Times*, Pacific Magazine Section Cover Story..

Nabhan, G. P. (2002). *Coming Home to Eat: The Pleasures and Politics of Local Foods.* New York: W.W. Norton.

North Central Initiative. (2001). *Attracting Consumers with Locally Grown Products.* Research report of the North Central Initiative for Small Farm Profitability. USDA-IFAFS. Download at: http://www.farmprofitability.org/local.htm

O'Hara, S., & Stagl, S. (2001). Global Food Markets and Their Local Alternatives: A Socio-Ecological Economic Perspective. *Population and Environment*, 22(6): 533-554.

Ostrom, M., & Jussaume, R. (2006). Assessing the Significance of Direct Farmer-Consumer Linkages as a Change Strategy: Civic or Opportunistic? In C. Hinrichs & T. Lyson (Eds.), *Remaking the North American Food System*, Lincoln: University of Nebraska Press.

Peirce, N. (2005, May 22). It's Mouthwatering: 'Thousands-mile Fresher' Food. *The Houston Chronicle.*

Pirog, R., Van Pelt, T., Enshayan, K., & Cook, K. (2001). *Food, Fuel and Freeways: An Iowa perspective on how far food travels, fuel usage, and greenhouse gas emissions.* Leopold Center for Sustainable Agriculture, Iowa State University, Ames, Iowa. Available at http://www.leopold.iastate.edu/pubinfo/papersspeeches/food_mil.pdf.

Pretty, J, & Lang, T. (2005). Farm costs and food miles: an assessment of the full cost of the UK weekly food basket. *Food Policy*, 30 (1).

Raloff, J. (2003). *Local Foods Could Make for Greener Grocers*, August 2, 164:5. Available at: www.sciencenews.org/articles/20030802/food.asp

Shuman, M. H. (1998). *Going Local: Creating Self-reliant Communities in a Global Age.* New York: Free Press.

Strauss, A., & Corbin, J. (1990). *Basics of Qualitative Research: Grounded Theory Procedure and Techniques.* Newbury Park: Sage.

Wilkins J. L., Bokaer-Smith, J.C., & Hilchey, D. (1996). *Local Foods and Local Agriculture: A Survey of Attitudes among Northeastern Consumers.* Survey Report. Division of Nutritional Science.

Wilkinson, K. P. (1991). *The Community in Rural America.* New York: Greenwood Press.

Rethinking local business clusters: the case of food clusters for promoting community development

Davis F. Taylor[a] and Chad R. Miller[b]

[a]College of the Atlantic, Bar Harbor; [b]Department of Economic and Workforce Development, University of Southern Mississippi, USA

> The business cluster concept is perhaps the most popular paradigm for studying and promoting local and regional economic development. While the business cluster literature acknowledges the existence of both locally-oriented and export-oriented clusters, research and practice places overwhelming emphasis on the latter. This paper examines two food-related business clusters, the Maine local produce cluster and the export-oriented Mississippi catfish cluster, to shed light on often-overlooked advantages of local business clusters. The Maine local produce cluster provides an "existence proof" that local clusters can be dynamic engines of local economic growth, and can have significant advantages over export-oriented clusters in terms of stability and resiliency. We call for further research to better understand the role of local-oriented business clusters in sustainable community development.
>
> **Keywords:** business cluster; local cluster; export oriented cluster; local food system

I. Introduction

The concept of business clusters, as originally popularized primarily by Porter (1990), has become one of the dominant perspectives used in local and regional economic development (Feser & Bergman, 2000; Rosenfeld, 1997; Waits, 2000). The study and promotion of business clusters, with their exemplary attributes of dynamic local firms, productivity-enhancing spillovers, concentrations of allied and supporting firms, efficient labor markets, and business culture connectivity, is seen as a means to stimulate local economic growth, increase employment, and raise income levels.[1] Given the well-established and multi-dimensional role of local economic activity in community development, the type of economic activities promoted in economic development literature and practice has significant implications for communities (Flora & Flora, 2008; Jackson, 1996; Shuman, 1998). The shape and dynamics of business cluster development impacts the solidarity and agency that is at the heart of community development (Bhattacharyya, 2004). This paper examines two food producing regions that previous studies identify as clusters in order to shed light on the important role agglomerations of businesses serving local customers can play in economic and community development.

Many applications of the business cluster concept make the distinction between clusters that are traded outside the region versus those that are traded within the region. In both types of clusters, firms involved in production are relatively closely located; the distinction is in regard to who are the consumers. Export oriented clusters provide goods and services for businesses and consumers beyond the immediate region, while local clusters provide goods and services for the immediate locality (Ketels, 2006). An examination of the literature on business clusters shows that the vast majority of attention by both researchers and development professionals is directed toward export oriented clusters. Prominent research such as Porter (2000) and Bergman (2007) only mention local clusters to contrast them with export oriented clusters, and our literature review identified very little research dedicated to local clusters.

The reason for inattention toward local clusters by business cluster researchers and practitioners is largely because export oriented clusters are seen as a means of stimulating local economic growth by bringing in revenue from outside the locality via the export activity; firms in the export oriented cluster grow either by tapping into expanding export markets, and/or at the expense of competing firms located outside of the locality. On the other hand, local clusters are seen as largely a zero sum game within a locality, as growth of some local firms comes at the expense of growth of other local firms; this is seen as less advantageous from the perspective of promoting local economic growth.[2] Further, these local clusters are not viewed as being innovative or productive, characteristics that are perceived as being crucial to competitiveness. Despite the acknowledgement that these local clusters account for the majority of regional employment, they are seen as providing lower paying jobs than traded clusters. In most research and practice, their value to economic development is primarily viewed via the nature, positive or negative, of their ancillary relationship to export oriented clusters.

Paradoxically, outside of the business cluster literature there is considerable research, activism, and practice focusing economic development efforts oriented toward local businesses that serve local customers (Barrios & Barrios, 2004; Estill, 2008; Kinsley, 1997). Proponents of locally-oriented economic development approaches such as "economic gardening" (as opposed to "economic hunting") and "LOIS" (locally-oriented import substitution) argue amongst other things that a local focus taps into a larger economic multiplier and creates a more stable economic base (Gibbons, 2008; Shuman, 1998). They argue that a local economic base largely composed of export oriented firms that are often recruited from outside the region can relatively easily leave the locality in search of lower operating costs elsewhere.

The purpose of this article is to use a business cluster approach to highlight aspects of local economic activity that are underappreciated in the dominant local and regional economic development literature. While existing business cluster literature establishes the high growth potential of export oriented clusters, we demonstrate that some local clusters also exhibit significant economic growth potential and are likely to have greater economic stability and make greater contributions to other dimensions of community development. We start by discussing definitions of clusters and identifying inconsistencies between common assumptions of how they are actually distributed in the economic and spatial landscape. We then examine two food-related clusters, the Maine Local Produce (MELP) cluster and Mississippi Catfish (MSC) cluster, providing respective case studies of a dynamic local cluster with positive implications for communities, and a declining export oriented cluster that is leading to severe regional community development challenges. Examining local food systems as clusters reveals additional overlooked characteristics and challenges assumptions about local clusters.

2. Business clusters: a closer look

According to business cluster theory and empirical analysis, business clusters form because co-located firms enjoy a wide range of economic advantages relative to firms that are geographically isolated from other firms in the same line of economic activity (Blair & Carroll, 2009). Despite some debate on nuanced terminology,[3] many researchers and practitioners generally accept Porter's (2000, p. 253) description of clusters as "geographic concentrations of interconnected companies, specialized suppliers and service providers, firms in related industries, and associated institutions (e.g., universities, standard agencies, and trade associations) in particular fields that compete but also cooperate." The cluster concept is based on the recognition that firms and industries are interrelated in both direct and indirect ways. They each contribute to a region's "collective efficiency"—that combination of external economies and joint actions that explain the higher returns that accrue to firms that are spatially clustered (Krugman, 1991). Well-known export oriented clusters include the Silicon Valley computing hardware/software cluster, the Detroit area automobile cluster, and the northern Italy small firm manufacturing cluster. The cluster concept has become the dominant paradigm for understanding how a region should approach and frame economic development. Local clusters, on the other hand, are thought to be found in many more localities than export oriented clusters, and serve local markets in industries that are not easily served by firms external to the region. Examples of local clusters could include auto repair shops, funeral homes, and beauticians, if the concentration of firms has a large enough mass to have allied and supporting firms, business connectivity and the other aspects of a Porterian cluster. These local activities can still be viewed as clusters, because the co-location of firms still provides some economic advantages, but the firms are generally not competing with firms outside the locality for the locality's customers.

Cluster identification

There are many different quantitative and qualitative approaches to identifying clusters, and our case study clusters from Maine and Mississippi are identified by several previous researchers who use various criteria. Several examples serve to illustrate the diversity of approaches to identifying business clusters: Mayer (2005) recommends a triangulation approach using location quotient, industry wages above national average, and a growth rate above the national average; Waits (2000) uses general indicators of business interdependence, concentration, significant size of rapid growth, and export orientation; Hill and Brennan (2000) use competitiveness, employment specialization, and indicators of export orientation (exporting to any location outside the region) to identify a cluster. An example of a qualitative determination is Britton (2007), who used extensive interviewing at the firm level to identify and designate a cluster. RTS, Inc. (2003) notes that rural clusters are particularly difficult to identify using conventional data. Using different methodologies to identify clusters precludes certain kinds of direct comparisons across clusters, but does not preclude examining general cluster structural, growth, and stability traits.

The export oriented/local cluster divide

The contention that export/traded/base activities generate new income for the residents of the economy and non-traded activities merely circulate income permeates economic development thought. A classic economic development textbook states:

> Local-sector activity is sustained by money brought into the area by the export sector. When the flow of money into the area from exports is equal to the flow of money out of the area for imports, the area's economy is in equilibrium. If the flow of money in exceeds the flow out, the economy will expand. If the reverse is true, it will contract. (Levy, 1981, p. 166)

Export oriented firms are deemed crucial because they stimulate local demand and thus create jobs in the local clusters, and are commonly perceived to have high economic multipliers[4] compared to typical local firms (e.g., retailers who buy most of their goods from China). A successful local economy, from this perspective, is one that can bring as much money as possible into the locality through exports, and minimize money being sent out of the locality through the purchase of imports.

However, an examination of local clusters within the findings of the influential Harvard Business School cluster mapping project (www.isc.hbs.edu/econ-clusters.htm), which includes a methodology of local cluster identification, reveals aspects of local clusters that are underappreciated by economic development researchers and professionals. In the Harvard project, local clusters are identified in the same manner as are export-oriented, on the basis of having a location quotient (LQ) greater than one, meaning that the locality has a disproportionate amount of the national employment in a given economic activity, relative to the region's share of economy-wide employment.[5] The Harvard Project authors write that "Local industries are those present in most if not all geographic areas, [and] are evenly distributed..." But this creates a mathematical conundrum: if local clusters were exactly evenly distributed, they would all have a LQ equal to 1. Local clusters being identified by having a LQ > 1 cannot be evenly distributed, because by definition the presence of a local cluster in a given region means that region has a disproportionate amount of employment in that economic activity. Local clusters being evenly distributed is like all students in a class being above the class average; given the way local clusters are designated, it is mathematically impossible. Quite predictably, when one compares actual local cluster maps generated by the Harvard project for two or more regions, one finds that some local clusters are present in some places, and not in others. Selecting a random example, Bangor, Maine, happens to have a local cluster in "local utilities," while Ann Arbor, Michigan does not; Ann Arbor has a local cluster in "local hospitality establishments," while Bangor does not. One locality may have a local cluster that is statistically absent in another region for at least several possible reasons: differences in demand, differences in labor productivity, path dependency, or simple statistical randomness.[6] This unequal distribution merits study and examination for potential community development opportunities.

3. Local food clusters and the Maine local produce cluster

The production, processing, distribution, and sale of local produce in Maine, along with firms providing support services for the industry, constitutes a local cluster. The MELP consists of interconnected companies (e.g., small farmers selling though farmers' markets), specialized suppliers (e.g., organic seed farmers and organic fertilizer producers), service providers, firms in related industries (e.g., grass farmers, specialty foods) and associated institutions. The MELP exhibits characteristics and dynamics that are contrary to commonly stated notions of local clusters, and thus serves as a useful case study in exploring the potential of local clusters as engines of local economic growth.

The Maine local produce (MELP) cluster's status as a growing local cluster is situated within the larger growth of local food production nationwide. In local food systems, producers generally seek to use as much local inputs as possible and target production for local consumers; such food systems are receiving considerable attention from a wide range of both popular writers (Kingsolver, 2007; McKibben, 2007; Pollan, 2006); and academic circles (cf. *Renewable Agriculture and Food Systems* and *Agriculture and Human Values*). Local food systems are contrasted with commodity food systems, in which farmers generally farm larger tracts of land, focus primarily on one to three crop plants, employ a much higher ratio of capital to labor, along with much greater quantities of petroleum-based fertilizers and pesticides. Such systems are associated with greater environmental damage, loss of farm employment, and narrowing farm profit margins (Lyson, 2007; Pollan, 2006). The interest in local food systems thus represents an anomaly: the researchers and practitioners of the business cluster concept are largely dismissive of local clusters, while others see distinct advantages to local clusters (though they do not always couch their discussions in the cluster concept), and there is a type of local cluster, local food clusters, that appears to be growing rapidly.

While a cursory examination of USDA statistics makes clear that commodity production of food products for export outside a given region still dominates the overall food system in the United States, there are also clear indications that locally-oriented food systems are growing rapidly. The number of farmers markets in the US has grown from 1755 in 1994 to 4385 in 2006 (Wholesale & Alternative Markets Program, 2006), and an estimated 19,000 farmers in the United States use farmers' markets as their sole outlet (USDA Agricultural Marketing Service, 2007). Community Supported Agriculture (CSAs[7]) have grown from an estimated 60 operations in 1990 to approximately 1100 operations in 2006 (USDA Agricultural Marketing Service, 2007). There are limited data available for a third major outlet in local food systems, local restaurants. However, the data available provide strong indications that this local economic activity is growing rapidly at the national level.

While defining "local" can be challenging (Ostrom, 2006), data and existing research indicate that Maine has a local food cluster. Colgan and Baker (2003) identify agriculture as a cluster in Maine using eight principal dimensions derived from Porter (2000), but they do not distinguish between commodity production for export and production for local use. The Institute for Strategy and Competitiveness (2008), on the other hand, identifies "local food and beverage processing" (a pre-established category for their nation-wide analysis) as a local cluster in Maine, based on LQ. While these two sources are somewhat equivocal regarding the localness of agricultural production in Maine, other data and research clearly identify that production for local consumption plays a disproportionately large role in agriculture in Maine. Smith (2004), while placing Maine farms on a continuum between commodity and local production, breaks down Maine's agricultural activity (including processing and distribution) into a commodity component representing $1.4 billion of economic activity and a local component representing $3.3 billion in economic activity; while commodity agriculture still provides similar farm sales ($419 million versus about $435 million for local production, in 2001 dollars), the local system dwarfs the commodity system economically on account of vastly larger amounts of local processing, distribution, and retailing activities.

Most significantly in identifying the MELP as a local cluster, Smith, Bell and Files (2004) undertook an extensive survey-based study of farm operations in Maine, to determine to what extent "sustainable agriculture" is practiced in Maine. In their study, 48% of responding farmers identify themselves as using sustainable agricultural practices as their dominant mode of production, while the remainder of self-identified respondents are classified as commodity producers, mostly for export. Subsequently within the study, sustainable agriculture farmers self identified as having a predominantly local focus in their marketing efforts, while commodity farmers are much more likely to sell to wholesalers. Thus, agricultural production and distribution in Maine has a much more local focus than it does in the United States in general.

Not surprisingly, local food production in Maine has the institutional characteristics associated with cluster development (local or otherwise) cited in the definition provided above from Porter (2000). The Maine Organic Farmers and Gardeners Association (MOFGA) is the oldest and largest state organic farming organization in the country; while "organic" is not the same as "local," the organization's cultural orientation is clearly toward local production. Also, the University of Maine has had a program in sustainable agriculture (which places a strong emphasis on local production and consumption) since 1988, long before local food systems gained their current prominence. Maine's tradition of inexpensive land as well as geographic and economic position on the fringes of US agriculture suggests a historical path that supported the growth of a local production agriculture cluster.

All of these characteristics lead us to designate the MELP as a local cluster. While the disaggregated data necessary to calculate a numerical LQs for local food clusters are not available, Maine agriculture's intensely local focus, relative to agriculture in the US in general, strongly suggests that employment in local produce production as a percentage of overall employment in the state is much higher than the same percentage in the United States (thus implying $LQ > 1$), so that Maine has a local produce cluster with Porterian cluster attributes and cost advantages.

Furthermore and most significantly, the MELP is an example of a type of local cluster that, contrary to the assumptions regarding local clusters in the economic development literature, exhibits strong economic growth. Smith (2004), as part of a larger assessment of Maine's social, demographic, and economic recent past and future prospects, sees local production as the future engine of growth in Maine agriculture. He cites data from the USDA Economic Research Service that shows that Maine's leading commodity crop, potatoes, has been in continual decline (in farm cash receipts) since the early 1970's, while more locally oriented vegetable production has nearly doubled in value in the same period.[8] The USDA Agricultural Census (2009) shows that small farm income in Maine is increasing and new career changers are being attracted to the MELP (Bander, 2009). The MELP is demonstrating economic growth, innovation (e.g., new organic crops and techniques), and productivity (e.g., adopting organic fertilizers that have greater long-run efficiency than synthetic fertilizers), showing that these important attributes are not limited to export oriented clusters.

4. Export food clusters and the Mississippi Catfish cluster

In contrast to Maine's local food cluster, the Mississippi catfish industry is an export oriented food cluster. The Mississippi catfish (MSC) cluster consists of firms involved in raising, processing, distribution, and marketing of catfish products and businesses providing support services for the industry. The MSC was purposely developed and flourished briefly in an economically distressed area, but now appears to be unsustainable, due in large part to its export-oriented features. While the economic sustainability of an export oriented cluster is a common theoretical criticism of this approach to economic development (Karlsson, Johansson, & Stough, 2005; Maggioni, 2004; Tichy, 1998) there has not been extensive empirical examination of this facet of export oriented clusters to rationally balance the panegyric literature that energetically promotes cluster-based economic development.

The MSC has been classified as a cluster using several different approaches. Barkley & Henry (1997) used a Gini coefficient approach for two-digit Standard Industrial Classification (SIC) industries, while Rosenfeld (2009) defines the cluster based on common products from a geographically limited critical mass of interdependent companies. According to the Mississippi Department of Agriculture (2007), at its peak Mississippi contained 400 catfish related businesses on 100,000 water acres, producing 60% of the US catfish, providing 13,000 jobs.

The MSC is often held up as an example of a successful rural industrial cluster, stimulating economic activity in a persistent poverty area (Barkley & Henry, 1997). However, increased global competition from other catfish clusters have put this important agricultural agglomeration in peril and exposed an inherent weakness of export oriented clusters in general. The desire of the farmers of northwest Mississippi, southeast Arkansas, and central Alabama to find agricultural alternatives for traditional export commodities intersected with the diffusion of innovation of new aquaculture techniques to begin the catfish cluster in the 1960s (Hargreaves, 2002). The alluvial soil and low water table of the Mississippi Delta are particularly suitable for catfish aquaculture, and this became the epicenter of the industry. In the 1980s, catfish production more than doubled in size, while interconnected companies (e.g., catfish farms, processors), specialized suppliers, (e.g., hatcheries, feed mills that make floating feed) service providers (e.g., live fish haulers, pond builders), firms in related industries (e.g., rendering plants, shrimp farms) generally grew. As with the MELP, the MSC developed associated institutions such as the Catfish Institute and the Thad Cochrane National Warmwater Aquaculture Center, and even a world catfish festival (Wellborn, 1983). By the 1990s, catfish production represented the largest dollar value of the whole aquaculture industry, with Mississippi accounting for approximately 50% of the total US catfish production (Dean, Hanson & Murray, 2003).

Catfish production in Mississippi is done on a commodity scale and is characterized by large, intensive pond systems. The average Delta catfish farm is over 400 acres, with an average pond size of twenty acres (Mott & Brunson, 1995). The high capital investment and operating capital requirements of commercial catfish production combined with low margins, as well as economies of scale, have prevented most small-scale farmers from participating in this enterprise although small-scale direct marketing is feasible (Stone, 1995). Mississippi's annual production of catfish of approximately $250 million was not a particularly profitable business (Gillette, 2004) so the industry was not in a strong position for the start of the "catfish war" with imported Asian catfish. Starting in the 1990s, the Vietnamese began developing fish breeding, feeding, processing, feed processing, byproduct processing, and waste treatment systems (Anbumozhi, 2007). When the US began lifting its economic embargo, the Vietnamese soon captured 20% of the approximately $590 million US market for catfish, driving down prices (Lam, 2003). "It is unclear what can replace catfish as easily as catfish replaced cotton. Attempts to make a tourist industry out of the fact that the delta was the birthplace of the blues are still embryonic. 'If we don't do something, there will be nothing but tumbleweeds here,' Jimmy Donahoo, a former catfish farmer, said. He, like others in the industry, thinks the producers should be supported by government subsidies, just like other farmers" (Streitfeld, 2008, p. B1). Thus, MSC exemplifies the potential instability of an export oriented cluster.

5. Analysis and conclusions: local cluster potential

The MELP represents a particularly striking "existence proof" of the potential positive economic impacts of local cluster development. Most significantly, the cluster shows strong economic growth, while capturing many more dollars of economic activity via processing, distribution, and retailing. The assumption that economic development efforts directed toward firms in a local cluster represents a zero-sum game within the region need not hold if demand for such local services is growing or other economic opportunities are emerging. From a broader perspective, there is no *a priori* reason to expect that innovation and the forces of creative destruction, whereby economic change creates new economic opportunities, technology, and growth while destroying older firms and modes of production (Schumpeter, 1950), do not exist for locally provided goods and services as well as export-oriented goods and service. A constantly changing local economic landscape provides continual opportunities for local entrepreneurs to identify and exploit opportunities for economic growth. In fact, Smith (2004) cites declining opportunities in commodity agriculture as a primary impetus for the growth of the MELP.

Apart from economic growth opportunities, local clusters may also be more economically stable, relative to export-oriented clusters. Unlike export oriented clusters, local clusters consist of lines of business that serve local consumers, usually in relatively small-scale, face-to-face contexts (Shuman, 2006); as such, they face little competition from similar clusters in other regions. While one never can know what distribution technology might hold for the future, it seems very unlikely that the MELP cluster will ever compete significantly with other local food clusters for the dollars of their local consumers. Likewise, those within the MELP cluster need not fret should Vermont and New Hampshire seek to enlarge their local food clusters. On the other hand, export-oriented clusters must always fear competition from similar clusters located outside of the region, as illustrated by the MSC cluster. The MSC cluster illustrated how export-oriented clusters can be economically threatened just as rapidly as they grew.[9] Lastly, while one can imagine some firms in some kinds of local clusters "growing out" of a local cluster and economy (e.g., a successful local auto repair shop evolves into a national chain), at least in the case of local food clusters this is not a realistic possibility. Brown (2002) surveys a broad range of research that consistently indicates that consumers patronize farmers markets first and foremost because of the superior quality of the produce relative to that found at regular large-scale supermarkets; assuming that this quality is in large part due to the locally-produced food being fresher and not bred for commodity storage and long-distance travel, in essence, it is being local that is the essential characteristic and competitive advantage of the cluster. Successful farms oriented toward local production may build on that success by further expanding their local production (say, into other crops), but they are very unlikely to "grow out" of MELP-like local production and "grow into" MSC-like export-oriented commodity producers, because it is being local that is the defining characteristic of the production. (Lyson, 2007). This rootedness in both customer value and production techniques suggests that local food clusters are less likely to exhibit high firm mobility that Shuman (1998) and Gibbons (2008) associate with export oriented economic activity.

There is at least one caveat to the proposition that local clusters face less competition from outside the region than do export-oriented clusters; this caveat in turn suggests one further way in which simple dismissal of local clusters as engines of economic growth can be short-sighted. Consider the MELP: one could imagine Maine seeking to maintain its apparent advantage in local foods, as this advantage not just provides for local consumers, but also can contribute to the cachet of living in or visiting Maine. If this becomes the case, there could be what amounts to a hybrid cluster: a cluster that is locally traded, but is larger and/or more efficient than similar local clusters in other regions, *such that the local cluster becomes part of the export-oriented activities*, in this case of resident recruitment/retention and tourism. Of course, economic development professionals have long been aware of the potential of unique, local features as engines of economic growth; that many of these features are couched within local clusters again suggests that local clusters merit closer attention than given in the business cluster literature.

The idea of local clusters being magnets for resident recruitment/retention and tourism leads to one final rationale for increased attention on local clusters. Supporting strong local clusters in emerging economic activities can contribute to desirable community characteristics, beyond direct economic development. A full and rigorous examination of the broad range of indirect economic benefits and non-economic benefits of local clusters is beyond the scope of this paper, but we offer here some initial possibilities. First, simple logic suggests that "growing" local clusters improves the provision of goods and services within a region, thereby presumably increasing the desirability of living in a place; supporting export-oriented clusters, on the other hand, benefits widely distributed consumers hundreds or thousands of miles away, therefore having no similar effect. Furthermore, strong local food clusters, for example, are associated with building entrepreneurship, preserving open space, increasing retail space land values (Brown, 2002) and creating social capital across class and educational lines (Ross, 2006). There is evidence the provision of local food is attractive to customers that represent a wide range of socioeconomic backgrounds and political preferences (Stephenson & Lev, 2004).

In conclusion, the "existence proof" example of local food clusters suggests that local clusters are misrepresented in the cluster literature and the common perception of these clusters may distort their value to sustainable economic and community development. There is always the danger of over-romanticizing or ignoring various costs of local production (DuPuis & Goodman, 2005), but it nevertheless seems that local clusters deserve more nuanced attention from economic and community developers.

Further research and more specific data collection are needed to understand the full range of local cluster benefits, the dynamics of local cluster development and growth, and what types of local clusters other than local food clusters (e.g., agglomerations of community banks, which generally remained more solvent in the recent financial crisis) have the positive externalities exhibited by local food clusters.

Notes

1. It should be noted that these are idealized attributes and sometimes merely geographic concentrations of firms are alluded to as clusters (Martin & Sunley, 2003), but for this paper we are referring to Porterian clusters.
2. Further support for export oriented economic activities is provided by export base theory; summaries of this theory is provided by Lewis (1976), Pollard and Storper (1996) and Dawkins (2003).
3. Cluster, inter-firm networks, agglomeration, industrial district, and economic milieu are often used interchangeably, depending on the research field.
4. An economic multiplier is a number used to estimate the economic impact from an infusion of new money into a community and its circulation within the economy before leaking out of the the local economy (cf. Kay, 2002).
5. Location quotients are a common means of cluster identification, when sufficient data exist to form the statistic. For a full explanation of location quotients see Blair and Carroll (2009).
6. In any data set, the distribution of sample points around the sample mean is usually attributable to unknown factors; however, writers in the field of economic and business empirical analysis recognize a more fundamental "randomness." See for example Studenmund, 2000, p. 13.
7. In the general CSA model, consumers pay a given farmer a lump sum payment at the beginning of an agricultural season in exchange for weekly deliveries of a bundle of produce that reflects the change in output as the season progresses.

8. Conversion from nominal to constant-dollar values by the authors.
9. While the logic seems strong, we do not have empirical evidence of greater economic stability within local food clusters. We suggest this as an area for future research in our conclusion.

References

Anbumozhi, V. (2007). *Eco-industrial clusters in urban-rural fringe areas: a strategic approach for integrated environmental and economic planning*. Hyogo, Japan: Institute for Global Environmental Strategies.

Barkley, D.L., & Henry, M.S. (1997). Rural industrial development: To cluster or not to cluster? *Review of Agricultural Economics*, 19(2), 308–325.

Bander, J.A. (2009). Maine experiencing growth in new farmers. *Maine Organic Farmer & Gardener*, Summer, p. 11.

Barrios, S., & Barrios, D. (2004). Reconsidering economic development: The prospects for economic gardening. *Public Administration Quarterly*, 28(1), 70–101.

Bergman, E. (2007). *Cluster life-cycles: An emerging synthesis SRE-Discussion 2007/04*. Vienna: Institute of Regional Development and Environment.

Bhattacharyya, J. (2004). Theorizing community development. *Journal of the Community Development Society*, 34(2), 5–31.

Blair, J.P., & Carroll, M.C. (2009). *Local economic development: Analysis, practices, and globalization*. Los Angeles, CA: Sage.

Britton, J.N.H. (2007). Path dependence and cluster adaptation: A case study of Toronto's new media industry. *International Journal of Entrepreneurship and Innovation Management*, 7, 272–297.

Brown, A. (2002). Farmers' market research 1940–2000: An inventory and review. *Renewable Agriculture and Food Systems*, 17(4), 167–176.

Colgan, C.S., & Baker, C. (2003). A framework for assessing cluster development. *Economic Development Quarterly*, 17, 352–366.

Dawkins, C. (2003). Regional development theory: Conceptual foundations, classic works, and recent developments. *Journal of Planning Literature*, 18(2), 131–171.

Dean, S., Hanson, T., & Murray, S. (2003). *Economic impact of the Mississippi farm-raised catfish industry at the year 2003*. Starkville, MS: Extension Service of Mississippi State University.

DuPuis, E.M., & Goodman, D. (2005). Should we go 'home' to eat? Toward a reflexive politics of localism. *Journal of Rural Studies*, 21(3), 359–371.

Estill, L. (2008). *Small is possible: Life in a local economy*. Gabriola, BC: New Society Publisher.

Feser, E.J., & Bergman, E.M. (2000). National industry cluster templates: A framework for applied regional cluster analysis. *Regional Studies*, 34(1), 1–19.

Flora, B.F., & Flora, J.L. (2008). *Rural communities: Legacy and change* (3rd edition). Boulder, CO: Westview Press.

Gibbons, C. (2008). *Economic gardening: An entrepreneurial approach to economic development*. Retreived from http://www.littletongov.org/bia/economicgardening/ (July 31, 2008).

Gillette, B. (2004). Profitability remains elusive for Mississippi catfish farmers. *Mississippi Business Journal*, August 2–8, p. 16.

Hargreaves, J. (2002). Channel catfish farming in ponds: Lessons from a maturing industry. *Reviews in Fisheries Science*, 10(3), 499–528.

Hill, E.W., & Brennan, J.F. (2000). A methodology for identifying the drivers of industrial clusters: The foundation of regional competitive advantage. *Economic Development Quarterly*, 14(1), 65–96.

Institute for Strategy and Competitiveness (2008). *State of Maine, Specialization by Local Cluster, 1990–2004*. Retrieved July 31, 2008, from www.isc.hbs.edu

Jackson, W. (1996). Matfield Green. In W. Jackson & W. Vitek (Eds.), *Rooted in the land: Essays on community and place*. New Haven, CT: Yale University.

Kay, D. (2002). *Economic multipliers and local economic impact aanalysis*. Retrieved January 12, 2009, from http://www.cdtoolbox.net/economic_development/000149.html

Karlsson, C., Johansson, B., & Stough, R. (2005). *Industrial clusters and inter-firm networks*. Northampton, MA: Edward Elgar Publishing.

Ketels, C. (2006). Michael Porter's competitiveness framework—recent learnings and new research priorities. *Journal of Industry, Competition and Trade*, 6(2), 115–136.

Kingsolver, B. (2007). *Animal, vegetable, miracle*. New York: HarperCollins.

Kinsley, M.J. (1997). *Economic renewal guide: A collaborative process for sustainable community development*. Snowmass, Colorado: Rocky Mountain Institute.

Krugman, P. (1991). *Geography and trade*. Cambridge, MA: MIT Press.

Lam, T.D.T. (2003). US 'catfish war' defeat stings. Vietnam: Asia Times, p. A1.

Levy, J.M. (1981). *Economic development programs for cities, counties, and towns*. New York, NY: Praeger.

Lewis, W.C. (1976). Export base theory and multiplier estimation: A critique. *The Annals of Regional Science, 10*(2), 58–70.

Lyson, T.A. (2007). Civic agriculture in the North American food system. In C.C. Hinrichs & T. Lyson (Eds.), *Remaking the North American food system*. Lincoln: University of Nebraska Press.

Maggioni, M. (2004). *The rise and fall of industrial clusters: Technology and the life cycle of region*. Barcelona: Institut d'Economia de Barcelona.

Mayer, H. (2005). Cluster monitor: A guide to analyzing industry clusters in regional economics. *Economic Development Journal, 4*(4), 40–53.

McKibben, B. (2007). *Deep economy: The wealth of communities and the durable future*. New York: Times Book.

Mississippi Department of Agriculture and Commerce. (2007). *Mississippi agriculture commodity directory: Catfish*. Jackson, MS: Mississippi Department of Agriculture and Commerce.

Mott, D., & Brunson, M. (1995). A historical perspective of catfish production in the southeast in relation to avian predation, *Seventh Eastern Wildlife Damage Management Conference*. University of Nebraska-Lincoln.

Ostrom, M. (2006). Everyday meaning of "local food": views from home and field. *Journal of the Community Development Society, 37*(1), 1–15.

Pollan, M. (2006). *The omnivore's dilemma: A natural history of four meals*. New York: Penguin Press.

Pollard, J., & Storper, M. (1996). A tale of twelve cities: metropolitan employment change in dynamic industries in the 1980s. *Economic Geography, 72*(1), 1–22.

Porter, M. (1990). *The competitive advantage of nations*. New York: Free Press.

Porter, M. (2000). Location, competition, and economic development: Local clusters in a global economy. *Economic Development Quarterly, 14*(1), 15–33.

Rosenfeld, S.A. (1997). Bringing business clusters into the mainstream of economic development. *European Planning Studies, 5*(1), 3–23.

Ross, N.J. (2006). How civic is it? Success stories in locally focused agriculture in Maine. *Renewable Agriculture and Food Systems, 21*(2), 114–123.

RTS, Inc. (2003). *Snapshots of Rural Innovation: A Compendium of Rural Cluster Vignettes*. Retrieved October 12, 2009, from http://www.hhh.umn.edu/centers/slp/reports.html

Schumpeter, J. (1950). The process of creative destruction. In J. Schumpeter (Ed.), *Capitalism, Socialism and Democracy* (3rd edition). London: Allen and Unwin.

Shuman, M. (1998). *Going local: Creating self-reliant communities in a global age*. New York: Free Press.

Shuman, M. (2006). *The small-mart revolution: How local businesses are beating the global competition*. San Francisco: Berrett-Koehler.

Smith, S. (2004). Maine agriculture: Adapting to a more complex setting. In R. Barringer (Ed.), *Changing Maine: 1960–2010* (pp. 389–410). Gardiner, ME: Tilbury House.

Smith, S., Pamela Bell, & Andrew Files (2004). *Understanding the dichotomy between industrial agriculture and sustainable agriculture: Types and characteristics of Maine farms*. Orono, ME: Maine Agriculture and Forest Experiment Station.

Stephenson, G., & Lev, L. (2004). Common support for local agriculture in two contrasting Oregon communities. *Renewable Agriculture and Food Systems, 19*(4), 210–217.

Stone, N. (1995). *Small-scale catfish production: Introduction*. Pine Bluff, AK: University of Arkansas United States Department of Agriculture and County Governments Cooperating.

Streitfeld, D. (2008). As price of grain rises, catfish farms dry up. *New York Times*, p. B1.

Studenmund, A.H. (2000). *Using econometrics: A practical guide* (4th edition). Reading, MA: Addison Wesley.

Tichy, G. (1998). Clusters: Less dispensable and more risky than ever. In M. Steiner (Ed.), *Clusters and regional specialisation* (pp. 226–237). London: Pion.

USDA Agricultural Marketing Service. (2007). *Community supported agriculture (CSAs)*. Retrieved August 28, 2008, from www.ams.usda.gov/AMSv1.0/

USDA Agricultural Census (2009). *2007 Census of Agriculture Report*. Retrieved October 22, 2009, from www.agcensus.usda.gov/

Waits, M.J. (2000). The added value of the industry cluster approach to economic analysis, strategy development, and service delivery. *Economic Development Quarterly*, *14*(1), 35–50.

Wellborn, T. (1983). The catfish story: Farmers, state services create new industry. In *1983 Yearbook of Agriculture* (pp. 298–305). Washington, DC: US Department of Agriculture.

Wholesale & Alternative Markets Program. (2006). *National directory of farmers markets*. Washington, DC: US Dept. of Agriculture, Agricultural Marketing Service, Transportation and Marketing, Wholesale and Alternative Markets.

The influence of community capital toward a community's capacity to respond to food insecurity

Jessica Crowe[a] and Justin Smith[b]

[a]Department of Sociology, University of North Texas at Dallas, Dallas, Texas, USA; [b]Department of Natural Resource Sciences, Washington State University, Pullman, Washington, USA

For many Americans, purchasing or acquiring food is a minor inconvenience rather than a major obstacle that must be overcome. In the United States, 17 million households (14.6%) were food insecure in 2008. Confronted with this vulnerability, some communities are attempting to re-localize many food system activities in an attempt to provide for healthier and more sustainable (socially, economically, and environmentally) food alternatives. Despite this rising movement, little research exists that examines which community-level characteristics are associated with a community's capacity to respond to food insecurity. Using data collected on 540 communities in the Northwest and Midwest, I examine the relationship between community capitals and food options available to residents of small to mid-sized communities. Findings show that communities with values and beliefs conducive for community betterment (cultural capital) coupled with acting on those beliefs through participation in civic groups and networking with outside communities and organizations (social capital) are much more likely to have a variety of sources of food than communities with low levels of cultural and social capitals.

Introduction

For many Americans, purchasing or acquiring food is a minor inconvenience rather than a major obstacle that must be overcome. However, the latest (2008) figures show that for 17 million US households (14.6%), obtaining food was difficult at some point during the year and 6.7 million households (5.7%) were food insecure to the point that at least some members repeatedly experienced the sensation of hunger (Nord, Andrews, & Carlson, 2009). A considerable body of research on food security in the United States examines the determinants, outcomes, and consequences of household food insecurity and hunger (Alaimo, 2005; Olson, Anderson, Kiss, Lawrence, & Seiling, 2004; Rose, 1999). Risk factors that contribute to food insecurity in the United States are mainly individual characteristics, such as educational attainment, employment skills, housing status, food skills,[1] health insurance status, abuse, and past economic hardship (Alaimo, 2005). Other research examines the nutritional consequences of living in a "food desert," an area with limited access to food (Blanchard & Lyson, 2009). Blanchard and Lyson (2009) find that individuals who live in food deserts are less likely to consume fruits and vegetables than people who live in areas with greater access to food. Their study shows that community-level factors such as access to food influence the quality of one's diet. Therefore, research is needed to build theory applicable to communities in how to respond to the problem of food insecurity, and, in particular, limited access to food. Understanding the factors that increase a community's capacity to respond to food insecurity can better interpret individual, household, and regional actions.

A community capitals approach (Flora & Flora, 2008) can be theoretically useful in explaining how a community's stock of social, cultural, and human capitals are related to food accessibility at the community level. Previous research has used the approach to explain how different types of capital influence community development in general (Braden & Mayo, 1999; Williams, 2004), and economic development in particular (Crowe, 2006, 2008a, 2008b; Green & Haines, 2008; Sharp, 2001; Singer, 2000). Generally speaking, studies show communities who take an asset-building approach to development[2] are more likely to be successful in meeting the needs of the community (Flora & Flora, 2008; Green & Haines, 2008). The logic behind the community capitals approach is that it leads to results that can directly aid local government and economic development officials as well as lead to training of community leaders in methods shown to enhance community well-being.

Since food insecurity is a problem for over 17 million US households (Nord et al., 2009), the argument is made that communities who take an asset-building approach to development (i.e. planned efforts to building resources that can be used to reduce or prevent poverty and injustice) are more likely to have the capacity to respond to the need for food security. This paper suggests that higher levels of community capital, particularly social and cultural capital, are positively related to a community's response to the need for food security by increasing both the accessibility of food and the quality and sustainability of food. To evaluate this proposition, survey and secondary data detailing the level of community capital and variety of food sources are analyzed for 540 small to mid-sized communities in 10 Northwestern and Midwestern states.

Conventional versus alternative food networks

Busch and Lacy (1984) identify three dimensions of food security. The first dimension, availability, refers to producing enough food to adequately feed the entire population. Differing from availability is the second dimension, accessibility, which refers to the ability for individuals to be able to access enough food to avoid hunger. While enough food is harvested every year to feed the global population, the distribution of food is unequal with many individuals unable to purchase it, or if unable to afford it, access free food. The third dimension, adequacy, refers to the quality of food in its nutritional properties and its absence of disease and toxicities. With respect to accessibility, Campbell (1991) distinguishes between three different types of food sources: the normal food system (e.g. supermarkets and grocery stores), government food assistance (e.g. school lunch and nutrition programs for elderly such as meals-on-wheels) and private food assistance, such as food banks. The normal food system with its emphasis on standardized production processes responding to competition and efficiency is characteristic of the conventional food system.

In addition to the conventional food system, the contemporary food sector is witnessing an increase in "alternative" food networks. Alternative food networks are localized chains that emphasize relationships between producers and consumers, while addressing environmental, nutritional, and health concerns of the conventional food system (Sonnino & Marsden 2006). Alternative food sources such as farmers' markets, community gardens, community supported agriculture organizations, and farm-to-school programs provide locally grown, nutritious food that is "grounded in the principles of justice, democracy, and sustainability" (Community Food Security Coalition, 2010).

To insure food security, there is a need for both the conventional and alternative food systems in a given locale.[3] Current demand of foods and food preparations make it very difficult to solely rely on alternative food sources. For instance, sugar, an ingredient found in many dishes, is not local for most people in the United States as it requires a tropical or temperate climate for sugarcane to grow. However, complete reliance on the conventional food system narrows the quantity and quality of food sources that people can access. Thus it is important for communities to make accessible a range of both types of food sources to aid in food security.

Community capital and food security

As Anderson and Cook (1999) point out, developing a theory of food security at the community level has consequences for social policy and action. One necessary ingredient of conceptualizing a theory of food security at the community level is knowledge of indicators or best measures that are positively associated with the likelihood of a community responding to the problem of limited access to food. Anderson and Cook propose that potential indicators include economic/social system descriptors that affect the capacity for change. Assessing a community's level of capital can be an effective way at measuring a community's capacity for change. Generally speaking, communities have seven types of capital from which they can use to address their needs: cultural, human, social, financial, built, natural, and political (Flora & Flora, 2008). For the purposes of this study, we examine levels of three types of community capital: social, cultural, and human in relation to a community's response to addressing food insecurity (i.e. by providing a variety of food sources in the community) while controlling for built, geographical, and demographic characteristics of communities.

Social capital

While there are many definitions of social capital, Putnam (1995, p. 67) states that social capital refers to "features of social organization, such as networks, norms, and trust that facilitate coordination and cooperation for mutual benefit." Although early studies linked social capital to individual outcomes such as educational attainment (Coleman, 1988) and wealth (Bourdieu, 1979, 1980), later studies, led by Putnam (1993), began to link social capital to larger units such as nations and communities. Under Putnam's conceptualization, communities and even nations could possess a "stock" of social capital. He argued that communities that build a "stock" of social capital will have higher levels of community development.

Flora and Flora (1993) have tested this notion with their concept of an entrepreneurial social infrastructure (ESI). Communities with high levels of ESI are tolerant of different perspectives and have networks that bridge across different groups in the community as well as to other communities and state agencies. Communities that are tolerant of differing perspectives have access to a broader array of choices and are more likely to come to an agreement that benefits all groups than do communities characterized by conflict and intolerance (Coleman, 1957; Sharp, Agnitsch, Ryan, & Flora, 2002). Bridging social capital is expected to facilitate the flow of information, resources, and support within a community by assisting in the exchange of information among groups as well as connecting organizations within the community to the state.

Several studies show a link between high levels of social capital and household food security. Martin, Rogers, Cook, and Joseph (2004) find that household social capital and community-level social capital (defined as the aggregate of household social capital) are significantly associated with decreased odds of experiencing hunger. While Martin et al.'s findings are significant, their measure of social capital is more of a measure of individual trust and community sentiment. Likewise their measure is a proxy of social capital and does not measure bridging social capital that facilitates information flow among groups within the community and with outside organizations. It is important to capture bridging social capital as it reflects dynamism between different groups that is not captured by aggregating household units of capital. Civicness can also aid in food security. For instance, Molnar, Duffy, Claxton, and Bailey (2001) note that local churches play an important role in developing local food banks, while Hinrichs (2001) notes that farmers markets are often located on public property and market managers are often a member of another community organization or a local government official. Morton, Bitto, Oakland, and Sand (2005) find that even for residents of communities located in food deserts, those who live in communities with high civic structure are significantly less likely to be food insecure. Similar to the effects of social capital on household food security, it is thus reasonable to expect communities with higher levels of bridging social capital and civicness will be positively associated with providing a variety of conventional and alternative food sources to its residents than communities with lower levels of social capital and civicness.

Cultural capital

Cultural capital is the least tangible of a community's capitals. For Bourdieu (1986), cultural capital is found in three states. The embodied state of cultural capital refers to legacy. Communities can pass on their understanding of society and their role in it to the next generation through legacy. The institutionalized state represents culture that is learned in the academic setting. This includes culture learned through private and public schools, daycares, and colleges. Lastly, the objectified state of culture includes cultural goods, such as material goods as well as councils, foundations, and other mechanisms that produce or celebrate material objects. The objectified state of culture is similar to the definition of cultural capital provided by Flora and Flora (2008), which includes the values and symbols reflected in art, customs, language, and tangible items.

Studies on food insecurity in less developed and traditional societies show culture to have an effect. For instance, many of the cultural patterns that lead to food insecurity in women and children in less developed countries are connected to traditional religious beliefs and customs (Molnar 1999). Harris (1995) claims that more egalitarian values may reduce food insecurity in women and children as these values are passed on to their children. Culture can also help explain the lack of response of certain less developed societies to food insecurity. For instance, custom of the North African Berbers dictates it acceptable to beg for water or shelter but not for food (Harris 1995). "Cultural traditions thus shape the definition of human need and the mechanisms legitimately available to satisfy it" (Molnar, 1999, p. 491).

Cultural capital determines how we view the world, what we take for granted, what we value, what things we think we can change (i.e. Bourdieu's embodied state of cultural capital). In the case of the United States and other developed societies, great variety exists among communities with respect to values and the belief in the power of human agency. A strength of the asset-building approach is that residents and community leaders can think more positively about what their community can do to better the lives of its residents and others. Regardless of levels of education among residents, communities across the United States have used their cultural capital in a number of ways to seek positive change while others take a more *laissez-faire* approach to change. With respect to a community's level of response to food insecurity, communities with values and beliefs that are conducive for community betterment may be more likely to implement a greater variety of food sources and have a greater variety of nutritious and environmentally sustainable food sources than communities with values and beliefs that favor the *status quo*. Because embodied cultural capital is the most abstract state of cultural capital, one way to objectively measure cultural capital is to use a proxy for the objectified state. In small communities that may not have a vibrant arts scene (what most people tend to think of when referring to material cultural goods), one way to objectively measure cultural capital is to measure the number of recreational and social opportunities that exist within a community. Since most communities view recreational and social opportunities as a form of community betterment, communities that are able to implement a variety of recreational and social opportunities may have the values and beliefs conducive for other types of community betterment, such as lowering food insecurity. It is thus logical to expect that communities with more cultural outlets will be positively associated with providing a variety of conventional and alternative food sources to its residents than communities with fewer cultural outlets.

Human capital

Human capital includes characteristics of individuals that strengthen one's ability to earn a living and provide for one's community, family, and self-improvement. It consists of one's personal assets: health, formal education, skills, intelligence, leadership, and talents (Flora & Flora, 2008). While human capital consists of a variety of personal assets, Becker (2002) states that education and training are the most essential forms of human capital.

Studies show many aspects of human capital to be associated with food insecurity (Alaimo, 2005). Personal risk factors that can contribute to food insecurity and hunger at the household level include lower levels of educational attainment, poor health, economic hardship, and lack of food skills. While studies show human capital to affect food insecurity at the household level, little is known about whether or not aggregate levels of human capital influence a community's capacity to respond to the food needs of some of its residents. For communities located in developed nations, wealthier, more educated communities may not have a wide variety of conventional food sources as most citizens do not seek food from government or private sources. Programs such as meals-on-wheels and private food banks may not be available. It is thus logical to expect that communities with wealthier and more educated residents will be negatively associated with providing a variety of conventional food sources to its residents than communities with poorer and less educated residents. As a result, the small percentage of residents who are food insecure may actually be at a disadvantage for living in a wealthier, more educated community.

With respect to the alternative food system, some farmers' markets and community supported agriculture (CSAs) in the United States have targeted or served a mostly educated middle-class clientele (Hinrichs, 2000). DeLind (1993, p. 8) notes that niche products grown organically are "exclusive products for an exclusive set of customers." However, many of these niche products are produced and marketed to non-local customers and are frequently mainstreamed with conventional food. On the other hand, in her study of consumer support for alternative food sources in Ohio, Bean (2008) shows an opposite relationship between education and alternative food sources with highly educated individuals less likely to support organic and local food systems than individuals with lower levels of education. These mixed findings lead one to hypothesize that a more nuanced relationship exists between education and support for alternative foods.

Data and methods

Sample

Data for these analyses come from a survey of economic development leaders in small to mid-sized communities in 10 states in the United States – Washington, Oregon, Iowa, Missouri, Wisconsin, Illinois, Michigan, Indiana, Kentucky, and Ohio – conducted during the falls of 2006 and 2009. Between 2006 and 2008 Wisconsin had food insecurity below the US average, Missouri had food insecurity above the US average, and all other eight states had food insecurity near the US average (Nord et al., 2009). To construct the sample for this study, the sample was restricted to incorporated communities with a population between 1000 and 17,000. This yielded a sampling population of 2578 communities. A stratified random sample of communities was then taken from the sampling population, making sure to get a mix of rural and urban communities, communities with different racial and ethnic demographics, and communities located throughout each state. In total 700 communities were sampled.

For each of the 700 communities, surveys were mailed to individuals knowledgeable about economic development in the community as well as other general aspects of the community. Positions held by participants included city mayor, city manager, chamber of commerce director, and economic development director. City clerks and local websites helped identify participants.

A mail survey was conducted using a modified Dillman method (Dillman, Smyth, & Christianson, 2008). Five contacts were made; however, the second contact was by email rather than mail. Since nearly all participants had access to email, attaching the survey to an email led to fast responses. Furthermore, some participants replied that another person was better suited to answer the questionnaire and subsequently forwarded the survey to that individual. A modified version of the surveys used by Flora, Sharp, Flora, and Newlon (1997) and Sharp (2001) in their analyses of economic development was used for the study. Completed surveys totaled 539, resulting in a 77% response rate. Table 1 reports means and percentage distributions for selected demographic and geographic variables by state.

Measurement of community capacity

Multiple methods were used to assess the capacity of a community to respond to food insecurity. Information on local food availability was first retrieved by means of a computer program that was developed to help streamline the data collection process. Using the PHP scripting language and a MySQL database, the program was designed to query Internet resources based upon longitude, latitude, community name, and zip code. For sake of simplicity, the program was seeded with three websites – google.com, localharvest.org and eatwellguide.org – that served as starting points to initiate the webcrawl and data retrieval process. Search terms used in the application included: "Farmers Market," "Community Supported Agriculture," "CSA," "Food Bank," "Grocery Cooperative," "Food Coop," and "Roadside Stand." Web pages that matched one or more of these search terms were then indexed by web address and community name. An HTML interface was also developed that automatically generated indexed hyperlinks, allowing the user to click on the links to ensure the content was both relevant and accurate. Data collected through the websites were then verified by comparison with survey data asking community leaders whether or not the community had each food source. Data response categories are defined as $1 = $ yes and $0 = $ no.

Conventional sources

Three items represents conventional sources: whether or not the community had a food bank, a meals-on-wheels program, and a major supermarket. Conventional food sources are measured by the number of affirmative responses. Thus a score of three represents a community having all three types of conventional sources, whereas score of a zero represents a community without any of the types of conventional food sources.

Alternative sources

Four items represent alternative sources: whether or not the community had a farmers' market, a consumer food coop, a community-supported agriculture farm, and a community garden. Alternative food sources are measured by the number of affirmative responses. A score of four represents a community having all four types of alternative food sources, whereas a score of zero represents a community without any of the types of alternative food sources.

Independent variables
Cultural capital

Respondents were asked to indicate whether or not each of the following recreational or social opportunities exist within the community: annual festival or celebration, local bike trail, local arts theater, art or cultural events occasionally held

Table 1. Percentages and means for selected demographic and geographic variables by state.

	IL	IN	OH	MO	WI	MI	IA	KY	WA	OR
% urban	56	54	54	46	48	63	11	44	50	43
% Bachelors or higher degree	20	14	18	16	19	21	17	15	18	15
% Poverty	9.1	9.2	10.3	14.6	6.9	11.6	10.6	15.9	12.2	11.1
Household income	44,617	37,517	38,318	32,934	41,256	40,253	33,653	34,183	36,309	33,743
Population	7122	7191	6972	6018	6647	6858	6010	6091	4321	4529
n	72	67	68	74	69	46	18	25	50	50

Note: Means and percentages are for the sample communities. n = 539. IL, Illinois; IN, Indiana; OH, Ohio; MO, Missouri; WI, Wisconsin; MI, Michigan; IA, Iowa; KY, Kentucky; WA, Washington; OR, Oregon.

in the community, and local or state parks. Cultural capital is measured by the number of affirmative responses.

Social capital

Civicness. Respondents were asked to rank the level of activity for nine types of community organizations with respect to community improvement or economic development activities. Community organizations included economic development, chamber of commerce/downtown merchants, service and fraternal, women's clubs or societies, civic groups, city government, environmental, commodity or farm, and church groups. Response categories included 1 = no such group, 2 = not very active, 3 = moderately active, 4 = very active. An additive index was created by summing the responses to the nine items (Chronbach's alpha = 0.794). Following the creation of the additive index, a dummy variable was created based on the frequency variable. Communities in the third and fourth quartiles (above average levels of civicness) are coded as one, and communities in the first and second quartiles (below average levels of civicness) are coded as zero.

Bridging networks (within community). Respondents were asked to indicate how often different groups in the community cooperated for community betterment in the past five years. Groups included: men and women's groups, younger and older residents, different racial/ethnic groups, rural and townsfolk, newcomers and longtime residents, and different religious groups. Response categories included 1 = never, 2 = rarely, 3 = sometimes, 4 = often. An additive index was created by summing the responses to the six items (Chronbach's alpha = 0.839). Following the creation of the additive index, a dummy variable was created based on the frequency variable. Communities in the third and fourth quartiles (above average levels of bridging capital) are coded as one, and communities in the first and second quartiles (below average levels of bridging capital) are coded as zero.

Bridging networks (outside of community). Respondents were asked whether or not a group from the community visited another community to learn about its community development efforts, the community joined with other communities or counties in the past three years to address economic development issues, the community joined with other communities or counties in the past three years to address regional environmental issues, and the community belonged to the state chamber of commerce or downtown development association. Bridging networks with other communities is measured by the number of affirmative responses.

Human capital

Human capital is measured by the percentage of individuals over the age of 25 with a bachelor's degree or higher.

Background variables

Because the economy is a probable driver of food insecurity, a few variables were included in the analysis to control for these economic drivers. The 2008 US Census Business Patterns were used to calculate the change in the total number of work places in a state. This was used to control for a state's economy. The total number of establishments rose between 1998 and 2008 for eight of the 10 states in which communities in the analysis are located. However, Michigan and Ohio witnessed a decrease of approximately 6000 workplaces each over the past decade. With respect to the number of supermarkets and supercenters in a state, once again Michigan and Ohio had fewer combined supermarkets and supercenters in 2008 than in 1998 while the remaining eight states saw a rise in the number of supermarkets and supercenters during the same time frame. Thus communities located in either Michigan or Ohio are coded as one and communities located in one of the other eight states are coded as zero. A community's level of wealth is controlled for by including a variable that measures a community's percentage of individuals below poverty. A community's racial and ethnic diversity is measured by including a dichotomous variable for majority white communities (greater than 90% white = 1, less than 90% white = 0) (US Bureau of the Census, 2000). A community's natural capital is measured by a variable labeled natural circumscription, to control for the amount of physical space a community has available. Participants are asked whether or not the community had physical space available for new or expanded light industry, new or expanded heavy industry, new or expanded small retail or commercial business, or new or expanded large retail or commercial business. Natural circumscription is measured by the number of affirmative responses. Because the population size of communities varies from 1500 to 17,000, population size is included in the model. Data are provided by the US Bureau of the Census (2000) and are truncated into four categories. Categories include communities with between 1500 and 5000 residents, communities with between 5001 and 10,000 residents, communities with between 10,001 and 15,000 residents, and communities with between 15,001 and 17,000 residents. Level of density at the county level is also measured. Rural–urban continuum codes are provided by the Economic Research Service (2004). Categories include 1 = communities located in metro counties, and 0 = communities located in non-metro or rural counties.

Analytic strategy

The first stage of the analyses focuses on the descriptive statistics of each dependent and independent variable as well as a comparison of means for each food source. For the second stage of the analyses, hypotheses are tested by performing Poisson regression to assess how a community's level of social, cultural, and human capital are related to the capacity of a community to respond to food insecurity.[4] All dependent variables are underdispersed count variables. Poisson regression is used for count variables in which the variance is smaller than the mean (Hoffmann, 2004). Variance Inflation Factor scores for all of the independent variables were well under 6.0, suggesting little multicollinearity among the variables.

Findings

Descriptive statistics and bivariate correlations

Descriptive statistics and bivariate correlations for all variables included in the reported analyses are presented in Tables 2 and 3. On average, communities have a little over two of the three types of food sources: major supermarket, food bank, and meals-on-wheels program. While they only have a little over one of the following

Table 2. Descriptive statistics for all variables included in the analysis.

	Mean	Standard deviation	Minimum	Maximum
Conventional food sources	2.42	0.81	0.00	3.00
Alternative food sources	1.33	1.06	0.00	4.00
Cultural capital	2.99	1.03	0.00	5.00
Civicness dummy	0.42	0.49	0.00	1.00
Bridging networks (within community) dummy	0.47	0.50	0.00	1.00
Bridging networks (outside of community)	2.41	1.16	0.00	4.00
Percentage with bachelor's degree of higher education	17.53	10.42	1.90	69.70
Percent below poverty	10.60	6.19	0.40	35.70
Natural circumscription	3.30	1.02	0.00	4.00
90% or greater white dummy	0.75	0.71	0.00	1.00
Ohio/Michigan dummy	0.21	0.41	0.00	1.00
Population size	1.71	0.75	1.00	4.00
Metro dummy	0.50	0.50	0.00	1.00

local food sources: farmers' market, consumer food coop, community-supported agricultural farm, community garden. Turning to the independent variables of interest, communities have an average of three of the five types of recreational or social opportunities and an average of 17% of adult residents have a bachelor's degree or higher. As for the indicators of social capital, it appears that community organizations are on average moderately active in community improvement activities, on average different groups within the community sometimes work together for community betterment, and communities join with other communities to address an average of two of the four issues. As indicated by Table 3, both types of food sources are positively correlated with cultural capital and all three indicators of social capital. However, human capital is negatively correlated with the provision of conventional sources and has no correlation with the provision of locally sustainable sources of food. We now turn to the results of the Poisson regression analyses.

Poisson regression

Table 4 shows results from Poisson regression models that explore the relationship between the number food sources in a community and the independent and background variables. With respect to conventional sources, a community's cultural capital is related to capacity to respond in the expected direction; communities with high levels of cultural capital are more likely to have a variety of conventional food sources than communities with low levels of cultural capital ($\beta = 0.090, p < 0.001$). While cultural capital is positively related to conventional food sources, social capital does not appear to be related. A community's level of civicness, bridging networks among community members, and bridging to other communities is not significantly associated with the number of types of conventional food sources in a community. Level of education in a community is negatively related ($\beta = -0.006, p < 0.01$) to the number of types of conventional food sources; however, the percentage of residents below poverty is not related. Turning to the statistical controls, both population and natural circumscription are positively associated with

Table 3. Bivariate correlations.

		1	2	3	4	5	6	7	8	9	10	11	12
Conventional food sources	1												
Alternative food sources	2	0.344											
Cultural capital	3	0.248	0.295										
Civicness dummy	4	0.222	0.202	0.140									
Bridging networks (within community)	5	0.139	0.093	0.139	0.298								
Bridging networks (outside of community)	6	0.152	0.203	0.305	0.196	0.192							
Percentage with bachelor's degree of higher education	7	−0.236	0.000	0.186	−0.105	−0.109	−0.058						
Percentage below poverty	8	0.211	0.022	−0.078	0.153	0.131	0.030	−0.456					
Natural circumscription	9	0.311	0.179	−0.047	0.102	0.035	0.020	−0.336	0.135				
90% or greater white dummy	10	−0.047	0.020	−0.029	−0.139	−0.158	−0.055	0.049	−0.371	0.025			
Population size	11	0.136	0.141	0.228	0.046	−0.020	0.014	0.195	−0.107	0.159	−0.192		
Metro dummy	12	−0.214	−0.169	−0.031	−0.200	−0.093	−0.032	0.317	−0.430	−0.109	−0.011	0.078	
Ohio/Michigan dummy	13	−0.044	0.099	−0.042	−0.036	−0.060	−0.016	0.081	−0.059	−0.007	−0.060	0.073	0.084

Table 4. Poisson regression (with robust standard errors) of community capacity to respond to food insecurity

Independent variable	Conventional food sources	Alternative food sources
Cultural capital	0.090*** [9.8] (0.018)	0.183*** [20.4] (0.043)
Social capital		
Civicness dummy	0.054 [5.7] (0.030)	0.158* [17.2] (0.076)
Bridging networks dummy (within the community)	0.039 [3.7] (0.029)	0.020 [1.8] (0.075)
Bridging networks (outside the community)	0.012 [1.3] (0.013)	0.107** [13.2] (0.036)
Human capital	−0.006** [−6.5] (0.002)	0.001 [1.0] (0.005)
Percent below poverty	0.004 [2.0] (0.003)	−0.005 [−3.1] (0.009)
Natural circumscription	0.081*** [9.1] (0.019)	0.150*** [17.3] (0.041)
Population	0.049** [3.7] (0.018)	0.104* [8.0] (0.044)
Metro dummy	−0.062* [−6.0] (0.031)	−0.202* [−18.2] (0.085)
90% or greater white dummy	0.049 [4.7] (0.037)	0.080 [8.2] (0.091)
Ohio or Michigan dummy	0.004 [−0.0] (0.037)	0.246** [27.4] (0.078)

Note: Standardized percentage change appears in square brackets (unstandardized for dummy variables). Robust standard errors are in parentheses. *$p < 0.05$; **$p < 0.01$; ***$p < 0.001$.

the number of conventional food sources. Communities with larger populations and more space for growth have a greater variety of conventional food sources than communities with smaller populations and less room for growth. However, communities in metro counties have fewer types of conventional food sources than communities located in rural counties.

As for alternative sources, many of the same trends emerge. Specifically, communities with high levels of cultural capital are more likely to have alternative food options that are socially and environmentally sustainable than communities with low levels of cultural capital ($\beta = 0.183$, $p < 0.001$). In addition, the level of civicness and networking with other communities are related to the number of local food options in the expected direction, but bridging networks among community members is not significantly associated with the capacity to respond. As expected, communities with higher levels of civic involvement and close ties with other communities are more likely to have alternative food options that are socially and environmentally sustainable than communities with low levels of civic involvement and that do not network with other communities ($\beta = 0.158$, $p < 0.05$; $\beta = 0.107$, $p < 0.01$). As with conventional food sources, both population and natural circumscription are positively associated with the number of alternative food sources. Communities with larger populations and more space for growth are more likely to have local food options that are socially and environmentally sustainable than communities with smaller populations and that have less room for growth. Also communities in metro counties have fewer types of alternative food sources than communities located in rural counties. One major difference between the two types of food sources is that the education of a community's residents is negatively related with the number of conventional food sources but is not significantly associated with alternative food sources. While a community's education does not appear to be related to the number of alternative food sources in a community, communities located in either Ohio or Michigan were significantly more likely to have alternative food sources than communities in the other eight states.

Discussion

This article offers a theoretical argument regarding how, by expanding one's view of the assets available to a community, communities can respond to food insecurity. Rather than a focus on the lack of resources, by examining different assets of communities this study provides evidence for the capacity of people to collectively overcome challenges in their community. Relationships exist between the number of types of food sources in a community and a community's cultural, social, and human capital. First, the number of types of cultural outlets in a community is positively associated with both the number of types of conventional and alternative food sources. Since communities typically view recreational and social opportunities as a form of community betterment, these findings suggest that communities that are able to implement a variety of recreational and social opportunities possess the types of values and beliefs conducive for other types of community betterment, such as lowering food insecurity by creating or preserving food sources. Likewise communities with many active civic groups are more likely to have more alternative sources of food than communities with fewer active civic groups. Communities that network with other communities and state agencies are also more likely to have the capacity to respond to food insecurity by providing for a variety of alternative food outlets. Thus communities with values and beliefs conducive for community betterment (cultural capital) coupled with acting on those beliefs through participation in civic groups and networking with outside communities and organizations (social capital) have built assets in the community that are positively associated with the provision of food sources. These findings support Mills and Ulmer's (1946) pioneering study that showed communities that were civically engaged and possessed a culture conducive to community betterment resulted in higher levels of well-being and welfare for their residents.

However, while Mills and Ulmer (1946) attributed civicness to a highly engaged middle class, this study finds a relationship between the number of accessible food sources and cultural and social capital regardless of measures of education and poverty. In addition, the current study shows no relationship between community-level education and poverty rates and the number of alternative sources in a community while showing a *negative* relationship between the level of education of a community and the number of types of conventional sources in a community. In other words, highly educated communities have fewer conventional food options available than communities with less educated residents. While the communities in metro areas tend to have more highly educated residents than rural communities, this relationship holds when urban/rural typology is held constant. However, education and wealth of communities do not appear to be related to the number of types of alternative food sources a community offers. As alternative food sources are becoming more accessible (over 3000 farmers' markets existed in 2002), it may no longer be solely the more educated communities that provide for these sources of food. This may explain why the current study's results do not support other studies that associate alternative food sources with the educated and wealthy (DeLind, 1993; Hinrichs, 2000).

It is notable that economic factors at the state level do not appear to be related to the number of types of conventional food sources of local communities. As global competition has led US corporations to move to locations with reduced costs in order to maximize profits, many cities and communities have witnessed a change from a manufacturing to service-based economy (Bluestone & Harrison, 1982; Lyson, 2004). Communities located in states that have been hit harder economically than other states (as measured by a loss of businesses and industries since 1998) do not appear to significantly differ with the number of types of conventional food sources than communities located in states that fared better economically. Lyson contends that the effects of globalization may lead toward an increase in "civic agriculture and a relocalization of at least some production and consumption" (2004, p. 83). This study provides support for this notion as economic factors at the state level appear to be related to the number of types of alternative food sources of local communities. Communities in Ohio and Michigan (the two states in this analysis that have had a decline in total number of businesses and industries since 1998) are more likely to have alternative food sources than communities in the other eight states in the study. These states have also experienced a decline in the number of supermarkets and supercenters since 1998. The declining economy in these two states may lead for some local communities to seek alternative sources of food to help restore what was lost due to the forces of global competition or to prepare for future losses.

Unlike past work that focuses on the predictors and outcomes of household food insecurity, this study focuses on a community's capacity to respond to food insecurity. By operationally defining community level factors for which corresponding measures do not and cannot exist for individuals or households, this study helps to build theory applicable to communities in how to respond to the problem of food insecurity. In addition, this study contributes to a theory of community capacity by differentiating between two routes communities often take to secure a variety of food options: conventional food sources and alternative food sources. Knowing the factors that lead to a community's capacity to respond to food insecurity can influence actions taken to reduce food insecurity at the individual, household, and regional scales.

Despite the various strengths of this study, some limitations must be acknowledged. First, the indicators of social capital are measures of community leaders' perceptions of civicness and networking within the community. While the sampled respondents are very knowledgeable about how active various organizations are in the community, future research can analyze local network structures through network analysis to better understand the ways in which civicness does or does not fulfill a community's promise of responding to food insecurity.

This study is also limited by the sample used in these analyses. This study examines small to mid-sized communities in the Northwest and Midwest. Therefore, the findings must not be generalized to cities or to communities in other regions of the United States. There is a need for more comparative studies to better evaluate the robustness of the findings.

In spite of these limitations, a number of strengths in this study contribute to the literature on community capacity, food security, and community capital. While more individuals are food insecure in the United States today than in 1995, the year that data started being collected, this study speaks to the capacity of communities to make a variety of food sources available by either preserving existing food options or generating new food options. With more options available to residents that include nutritious, environmentally sustainable, and free food, fewer individuals will be food insecure. While many other factors at the national and individual levels influence food insecurity, this study shows that communities can enhance their cultural and social capitals to provide as many options of food sources as possible. Collectively, community residents can draw upon their assets and strengthen other forms of capital to create an environment that enables individuals and families to fulfill their basic food needs.

Notes

1. Food skills include actions that individuals can take that result in acquiring inexpensive, nutritious food. This includes growing, collecting, and preserving one's own food as well as buying fresh produce in bulk and preserving.
2. An asset-building approach to development is defined as planned efforts to building resources that individuals, organizations, or communities can use to decrease or prevent poverty and other injustices such as food insecurity.
3. Indeed several scholars (e.g., Murdoch & Miele, 1999; Sonnino & Marsden, 2006) assert that in some cases no clear boundaries exist between conventional and alternative food systems. Such is the case for large producers of eggs that alongside the standardized egg produce an "animal-friendly" version of eggs targeted toward specific consumers.
4. A limitation of cross-sectional data is the uncertainty of causation. While Poisson regression analyses can reveal correlations between the dependent and independent variables, caution must be taken in asserting causality from data collected from one point in time. Nevertheless, various forms of community capital theory assert that building community assets influence community development and not *vice versa*. Because the study's hypotheses were made prior to data collection, I infer causal relationships, albeit with caution.

References

Alaimo, K. (2005). Food insecurity in the United States: An overview. *Topics in Clinical Nutrition*, 20, 281–298.

Anderson, M., & and Cook, J. (1999). Community food security: Practice in need of theory? *Agriculture and Human Values*, 16, 141–150.

Bean, M. (2008). *Consumer support for local and organic foods in Ohio* (Dissertation). The Ohio State University.

Becker, G.S. (2002). Human capital. In *The concise encyclopedia of economics*. Retrieved from http://www.econlib.org/library/Enc/HumanCapital.html

Blanchard, T., & Lyson, T. (2009). Retail concentration, food deserts, and food disadvantaged communities in rural America. Retrieved from http://srdc.msstate.edu/ridge/files/recipients/02_blanchard_final.pdf

Bluestone, B., & Harrison, B. (1982). *The deindustrialization of America*. New York: Basic Books.

Bourdieu, P. (1979). Les trois etats du capital culturel. *Actes de la Recherche en Sciences Sociales*, 31, 3–6.

Bourdieu, P. (1980). Le capital social: Notes provisoires. *Actes de la Recherche en Sciences Sociales*, 31, 2–3.

Bourdieu, P. (1986). The forms of capital. In: J.C. Richardson (Ed.), *Handbook of theory and research for the sociology of education* (pp. 241–258). New York: Greenwood Press.

Braden, S., & Mayo, M. (1999). Culture, community development, and representation. *Community Development Journal*, 34, 191–204.

Busch, L., & Lacy, W. (1984). *Food security in the United States*. Boulder, CO: Westview Press.

Campbell, C. (1991). Food insecurity: A nutritional outcome or a predictor variable. *Journal of Nutrition. Symposium: Nutritional Assessment and Intervention*, 121, 408–415.

Coleman, J. (1957). *Community conflict*. Glencoe, IL: Free Press.

Coleman, J. (1988). Social capital in the creation of human capital. *American Journal of Sociology*, *94*, S95–S120.

Community Food Security Coalition. (2010). About CSFC. Retrieved from http://www.foodsecurity.org/

Crowe, J. (2006). Community economic development strategies in rural Washington: Toward a synthesis of natural and social capital. *Rural Sociology*, *71*, 573–596.

Crowe, J. (2008a). The role of natural capital on the pursuit and implementation of economic development. *Sociological Perspectives*, *51*, 827–851.

Crowe, J. (2008b). Economic development in the nonmetropolitan west: The influence of physical, natural, and social capital. *Community Development: Journal of the Community Development Society*, *39*, 51–70.

DeLind, L. (1993). Market niches, "cul de sacs", and social context: Alternative systems of food production. *Culture and Agriculture*, *47*, 7–12.

Dillman, D., Smyth, J., & Christianson, L. (2008). *Internet, mail, and mixed-mode surveys: The tailor design method* (3rd ed.). New York: Wiley Publishing.

Economic Research Service. (2004). *County typology codes*. Washington, DC: US Department of Agriculture.

Flora, C., & Flora, J. (1993). Entrepreneurial social infrastructure: A necessary ingredient. *The Annals of the American Academy of Political and Social Sciences*, *529*, 48–58.

Flora, C., & Flora, J. (2008). *Rural communities: Legacy and change* (3rd ed.). Boulder, CO: Westview Press.

Flora, J., Sharp, J., Flora, C., & Newlon, B. (1997). Entrepreneurial social infrastructure and locally initiated economic development in the nonmetropolitan United States. *The Sociological Quarterly*, *38*, 623–645.

Green, G., & Haines, A. (2008). *Asset building and community development* (2nd ed.). Thousand Oaks, CA: Sage Publications.

Harris, B. (1995). The intrafamily distribution of hunger in South Asia. In: J. Dreze, A. Sen, & A. Hussain (Eds.), *The political economy of hunger* (pp. 224–297). New York: Oxford University Press.

Hinrichs, C. (2000). Embeddedness and local food systems: Notes on two types of direct agricultural market. *Journal of Rural Studies*, *16*, 295–303.

Hinrichs, C. (2001). Observations and concerns of Iowa farmers' market managers: Summary of research findings. Retrieved from http://www.soc.iastate.edu/extension/bulletins.html

Hoffmann, J.P. (2004). *Generalized linear models: An applied approach*. Boston: Pearson Education Incorporation.

Lyson, T. (2004). *Civic agriculture: Reconnecting farm, food, and community*. Medford, MA: Tufts University Press.

Martin, K., Rogers, B., Cook, J., & Joseph, H. (2004). Social capital is associated with decreased risk of hunger. *Social Science and Medicine*, *58*, 2645–2654.

Mills, C.W., & Ulmer, M. (1946). *Small business and civic welfare*. Report of the Smaller War Plants Corporation to the Special Committee to Study Problems of American Small Business. Document 135. US Senate, 79th Congress, 2nd session, February 13. Washington, DC: US Government Printing Office.

Molnar, J. (1999). Sound policies for food security: The role of culture and social organization. *Review of Agricultural Economics*, *21*, 489–498.

Molnar, J., Duffy, P., Claxton, L., & Bailey, C. (2001). Private food assistance in a small metropolitan area: Urban resources and rural needs. *Journal of Sociology and Social Welfare*, *28*, 187–209.

Morton, L., Bitto, E., Oakland, M.J., & Sand, M. (2005). Solving the problems of Iowa food deserts: Food insecurity and civic structure. *Rural Sociology*, *70*, 94–112.

Murdoch, J., & Miele, M. 1999. Balck to nature: Changing 'worlds of production' in the food sector. *Sociologia Ruralis*, *39*, 465–483.

Nord, M., Andrews, M. & Carlson, S. (2009). *Household food security in the United States, 2008*. Washington, DC: US Department of Agriculture.

Olson, C., Anderson, K., Kiss, E., Lawrence, F., & Seiling, S. (2004). Factors protecting against and contributing to food insecurity among rural families. *Family Economics Nutrition Review*, *16*, 12–20.

Putnam, R. (1993). *Making democracy work: Civic traditions in modern Italy*. Princeton, NJ: Princeton University Press.

Putnam, R. (1995). Bowling alone: America's declining social capital. *Journal of Democracy, 6*, 66–78.

Rose, D. (1999). Economic determinants and dietary consequences of food insecurity in the United States. *Journal of Nutrition, 129*, 517S–520S.

Sharp, J. (2001). Locating the community field: A study of interorganizational network structure and capacity for community action. *Rural Sociology, 66*, 403–424.

Sharp, J., Agnitsch, K., Ryan, V., & Flora, J. (2002). Social infrastructure and community economic development strategies: The case of self-development and industrial recruitment in rural Iowa. *Journal of Rural Studies, 18*, 405–417.

Singer, M. (2000). Culture works: Cultural resources as economic development tools. *Public Management, 8*, 11–16.

Sonnino, R., & Marsden, T. (2006). Beyond the divide: Rethinking relationships between alternative and conventional food networks in Europe. *Journal of Economic Geography, 6*, 181–199.

US Bureau of the Census. (2000). *Summary file 1*. Washington, DC: Author.

Williams, L. (2004). Culture and community development: Towards new conceptualizations and practice. *Community Development Journal, 39*, 345–359.

Localizing Linkages for Food and Tourism: Culinary Tourism as a Community Development Strategy

Gary Paul Green and Michael L. Dougherty

The local food movement is taking a variety of forms--including farm-to-school programs, farmers markets, community supported agriculture, and direct marketing. An emerging component of this movement is culinary tourism. Culinary tourism offers new opportunities for communities to integrate tourism and local food systems in order to promote economic development, respond to the demand for quality food and dining experiences, and build on the cultural heritage of the region. This paper examines culinary tourism through a case study of the Kingdom So Delicious program in Door County, Wisconsin. This analysis is based on intensive interviews with owners/managers of four restaurants and surveys of 30 retailers and 40 farmers in the region. Retail establishments relied heavily on local produce, largely due to a commitment to help local producers. Farmers frequently combined marketing fresh food to local retail establishments with sales to wholesalers. The most frequently cited concerns with producing for local establishments involved in culinary tourism were low prices and challenging logistics. The lessons of this study are not limited to Door County but can be applied to other, similar communities seeking to strengthen culinary tourism.

The local food movement offers new economic opportunities for small and medium-sized farms, reduces their environmental footprints, and promotes good nutrition among consumers (Kloppenburg, Lezberg, Demaster, Stevenson, & Hendrickson, 2000). Local food systems take a variety of forms, including farm-to-school programs, farmers markets, and community supported agriculture. An emerging component of this movement is food and cultural tourism, which is often referred to as culinary tourism (Long, 2004). Culinary tourism emphasizes unique foods and dishes from the culture of the host region. Many regions, for example, feature their wine industries as a focal point of their tourism programs. The Missouri Regional Cuisines Project is a recent effort to promote a group of wineries in Eastern Missouri. Other regions promote their local cuisine or other agricultural products in which they have a comparative advantage as tourist attractions. These projects are often promoted as "trails" with businesses of various types in a geographic region offering complementary culinary and cultural experiences for visitors. The state of Minnesota has an elaborate trail system that focuses on culinary experiences. Although there are a growing number of states promoting culinary tourism to address the waning economic

---

Gary Paul Green and Michael L. Dougherty. We appreciate the assistance of Dean Volenberg.

vitality of many rural areas, there is very little research that has examined the effects of these programs for farmers and rural economic development. This paper evaluates some of the supply and demand issues surrounding local foods in a culinary tourism market, and examines how communities overcome some of the institutional barriers to building the local food systems that constitute the primary input into culinary tourism.

According to the Travel Industry Association (2007), 27 million travelers, or 17 percent of American leisure travelers, engaged in culinary or wine-related activities between 2003 and 2006. Culinary tourists have a significant impact on regional economies and spend about $1,000 per trip. The Travel Industry Association projects tremendous growth for the culinary traveler market, as the share of U.S. leisure travelers interested in culinary travel in the near future (60 percent) is significantly larger than those currently engaged. This projected growth in culinary travel brings opportunities for economic development to rural America, along with challenges for farmers, ranchers, restaurateurs, and communities seeking to maintain their rural character and agrarian authenticity. Given the size of the rural tourism industry and its potential for sustainable development, it is vastly under-analyzed in the academic literature.

Culinary tourism projects present several interesting issues for community development planning. First, promoting a region as a tourist destination frequently requires coordination across several communities. There are clearly benefits to having a critical mass of this type of economic activity. Having a sufficient number of farms, restaurants, and retail establishments is a key to successful marketing. Given that political boundaries often do not coincide with these regions, equity in terms of revenues, taxes and promotions can be a problem.

Second, culinary tourism involves several sectors of the regional economy that frequently have little interaction: farmers/ranchers, retail establishments, restaurants, and processors. This organization may require new markets and institutions to build and maintain the supply of and demand for local foods in the region. Markets for local foods and beverages must be supported and developed. This may require new organizations and strategies among various actors in the local food system.

Finally, much of the research on local food systems has focused on the role of large institutions in purchasing local foods (Pirog, 2001). This literature suggests that the sizable demand by institutions, such as schools, prisons and universities is the major hurdle to building local food systems. These institutions require a large supply of produce on a regular basis. Farmers in most regions have a difficult time meeting quantity requirements and direct marketing is further complicated by the seasonality of production. Additionally, many institutions prefer to purchase processed foods to reduce costs. Culinary tourism may not have the same constraints. In most cases, quantity of demand is much lower with restaurants than in large institutions. Also, because demand is a function of tourism, it often follows the contours of the growing season, to some extent, as well. Finally, restaurants and retail establishments involved with culinary tourism are less likely to require processed foods for their needs. They have greater capacity to process food on an ad hoc basis.

There is a limited amount of research on the motivations for purchasing local food. Starr et al. (2003) suggests that local foods may have several advantages. Food buyers may switch to local products because the improved quality outweighs slightly higher prices. Another consideration, however, may be the role of social relationships in shaping purchasing decisions (Cowell & Green, 1994). Decisions about where restaurants and retail establishments purchase food may be influenced more by social relationships and commitment to help local farms than by profit maximization. Local businesses are not totally self-interested actors, but, instead, may base their decisions on what will benefit their family, friends and acquaintances. Part of the reason may be that merchants prefer to transact with people with whom they have developed trust over time (Granovetter, 1985).

Another reason is that they may prefer to contribute to the wellbeing of the community by supporting local businesses. Both of these motives, trust and support for local businesses, could be interpreted as examples of self-interest or ethical factors. For example, purchasing food from local farmers could be influenced by the desire to help out a friend or reduce transaction costs. It may be the case that organizations and institutions involved in local food systems will express both motivations in their decisions to get involved. In any case, the moral economy may play a bigger role in the development of culinary tourism than it might in institutional buying. The concept of moral economy implies that principles of fairness and equity can be applied to an economy system.

Culinary Tourism

Partially as a response to the growing concentration and centralization of the food system, prominent critics have promoted alternative food production and distribution systems over the past two decades (Pollan, 2006). A growing number of communities are developing farmers markets, farm-to-school programs, and community supported agriculture organizations (Allen & Guthman, 2000). For example, the U.S. Department of Agriculture estimates there are almost 5,000 farmers markets today, almost double the number ten years ago. Despite their popularity, local food systems face several common obstacles. One of the key limitations of many forms of institutional buying, such as farm-to-school programs, has been processing. Many institutions will purchase only processed goods. Most independent farmers simply sell their raw commodities on the open market.

Another major obstacle has been the issue of demand. The demand for local food is high and the supply is often seasonal. Because small farmers are most likely to participate in local food systems, it is difficult (and costly) to meet the demand for local food by restaurants, schools, institutions, etc. Most communities lack the institutional mechanisms to coordinate supply and demand for local food. This is not to say that there have not been successful programs. For example, the number of farmers' markets has grown rapidly over the past decade and avoids some of the obstacles that other forms of direct marketing face.

Culinary tourism, defined broadly as the pursuit of unique and memorable eating and drinking experiences, provides a way of linking local food systems with the tourist experience. Culinary tourism and agritourism can be distinguished in the following manner. Culinary tourism is a subset of cultural tourism and posits that food is an expression of culture. Agritourism is typically viewed as a subset of rural tourism and the focus is on-farm activities. Culinary tourism refers to activities both on and off the farm. Off-farm activities might include restaurants in a community featuring local specialties and foods on their menu. On-farm culinary activities could include visits to farms to learn how to prepare specialties that are indigenous to the region.

Culinary tourism has most often been associated with the wine industry. Several regions in the United States promote trails featuring regional wineries, and increasingly, breweries. Rather than marketing a specific locality, the entire region is promoted. Local breweries and wineries may offer tours and festivals. Restaurants may provide cooking classes on how to prepare regional foods. Retail establishments sell raw and processed local foods and beverages. Local farmers may sponsor on-farm visits and tours as well as participate in direct marketing opportunities such as farmer's stands and U-pick operations. Tourists are increasingly looking for authentic experiences that take them "back to nature" (Bessiere, 1998). Experiencing local cuisine and regional culture is one way to meet this demand.

This paper examines the case of culinary tourism in Door County, Wisconsin to evaluate the lessons learned about this form of tourism. The central focus is on how markets are constructed and reproduced for local food. In other words, how do producers connect with buyers in the region? How is demand generated and sustained on the part of local food buyers? Much of the literature focuses on institutions in regional food systems and the role of intermediaries in linking demand with supply. Another perspective views markets as consisting of social relationships. Information and market behavior is shaped by these relationships (Fligstein, 2001). These social relationships play a role in guiding information and market contacts in the region.

Kingdom So Delicious

Door County is located in Northeast Wisconsin (the finger-like peninsula protruding into Lake Michigan). It has been a tourist destination for decades, especially for residents from the Chicago area who are attracted to the area for its classic farmscapes, abundant water and outdoor activities, and rich culinary traditions. Door County is known for several food products, such as cherries, apples, whitefish, and maple syrup, and these foods are tied to cultural traditions, especially the fish boil (a culinary tradition in the Great Lakes states that consists of large chunks of fish boiled with potatoes in a cast iron kettle). Local foods are often featured in restaurants, retail establishments and roadside stands. Door County and its cultural traditions received national attention in William Ellis' 1969 *National Geographic* article, "Wisconsin's Door Peninsula 'A Kingdom So Delicious,'" which sang the praises of Door County's history and tourism industry. Even in 1969, tourism was a 100 million dollar a year business in Door County.

In 2005, Door County developed a promotional campaign entitled *A Kingdom So Delicious*. The program is managed by the Door County Chamber of Commerce/Visitor's Bureau. The campaign is supported by a network of institutions including businesses, the Peninsula Arts & Humanities Alliance (PAHA), University of Wisconsin Extension, the Door County Economic Development Corporation (DCEDC), and several civic associations. *Kingdom So Delicious* promotes regional foods by creating "packages" for participating lodging establishments, dining establishments, and other sources of entertainment (e.g., theater and art galleries) that are linked with one another. This package creates many networks among area businesses of different varieties rather than a single, region-wide network. Additionally, a hefty program of events serves as an incentive for area restaurants to feature local foods in their dishes, and for art and theater venues to feature area history and culture-themed events. Food and beverage producers are encouraged to become involved by partnering with an art venue to offer combined art and cuisine events. One of the tools that the Chamber uses is a passport that includes a list of restaurants and retail establishments that tourists can visit. The "Passport" booklet is promoted within the Door County community itself including second home owners, as well as in the major nearby metropolitan areas of Chicago, Minneapolis, Milwaukee and Madison and is also available electronically on the Chamber's website.

The case study focuses on one of the most developed culinary tourism sites in the region. Local foods are an integral part of the culture and a central feature of the tourism industry in the area. Therefore, this case is optimal for assessing how producers and retail establishments have addressed some of the obstacles faced in building local food systems for culinary tourism. The fact that Door County is so unique complicates somewhat extrapolating lessons from this case to other rural communities. Nevertheless, there are important lessons to be learned.

Methods

The data for this analysis are based on mailed surveys to 83 retail establishments and 62 agricultural enterprises. Retail establishments may include restaurants, supermarkets, cooking schools, bakeries, wineries and inns. The retail establishments surveyed were selected for their participation in *A Kingdom So Delicious*. Retailers responded to questions about their purchasing practices, motivations underlying those practices, impressions of local agricultural production, and the changes that businesses have undergone as a result of purchasing local foods. Out of 83 surveys mailed to retailers, 30 responded (36 percent response rate). Of these 30, seven were retail shops, 17 were food service establishments, two were supermarkets, and 10 were in the "other" category, which included bakeries, bed & breakfasts, wineries, and cooking schools, among others.

To examine farmers' perspectives on the local market, a separate survey instrument was sent to 62 farms in Door County. This sample was drawn from a list of farmers in Door County who marketed directly to retail establishments in the region. The University of Wisconsin-Extension county agricultural agent provided the list. Of those 62 surveys there were 40 responses (64% response rate).

Finally, intensive interviews were conducted with four owners, general managers and head chefs of restaurants in the region. These restaurants were selected because they were the largest establishments involved in culinary tourism. These interviews provided several key insights into the demand for local foods in the region.

The results of the two surveys were analyzed separately creating individual charts and tables for each question. These charts were analyzed for inconsistencies, themes and stark findings, discarding the inconsistent data and isolating common findings between the survey and interview data. General findings are included in two technical reports that resulted from this research (Dougherty, Green, & Volenberg, 2008a, 2008b.).

The Demand For And Supply Of Local Foods

This analysis focuses on the factors influencing the organization of local food networks, or social relationships, for culinary tourism. Several questions are addressed: How much local food is purchased by retailers and restaurants? What factors influence their decision to buy locally? What are the primary obstacles to growing the local food system? On the supply side, there were several relevant questions: How many local producers sell in the regional market? Why do producers sell locally? What constraints do they see to expanding their sales in this market?

As previously mentioned, Door County possesses a robust and long-standing tourism industry. Tourism is the largest sector of Door's economy. Ninety three percent of respondents indicated that tourists comprised between 60 and 80 percent of their clientele.

Retail establishments and restaurants reported that a significant amount of their total food purchasing came from food that was sourced locally. "Local" for purposes of this survey was defined as food that was produced in Door or adjacent counties. In some cases, produce is grown locally, but processed outside the region. Most respondents considered this local food.

Approximately 24% of total fresh food expenses came from local sources. This figure was calculated by taking the mean figure for reported total food costs from local sources as a percentage of the mean figure of total food costs from all sources. The average total food costs, per establishment, for 2007, were $64,846.25 while the corresponding average spent on locally-sourced food was $15,434.88. Door County cherries and apples were the most popular items. The third most popular was wine, followed by fish, and then maple syrup. Each of these are food items that Door County is known to produce particularly well.

Respondents indicated that local products are comparable with non-local products in terms of blemishes, consistency of shape, and shelf-life, and durability. Local foods were deemed lacking in terms of packaging, handling, and delivery consistency. This information conforms to what respondents indicated were the most significant barriers to increasing the amount of food they sourced locally.

When asked about their motivation for purchasing locally sourced food, managers of restaurants and retail establishments were most likely to point to the importance of social relationships and the contribution to local businesses (Figure 1). Thirteen percent of respondents indicated that increased revenue was the main reason for adopting these practices and 19 percent of respondents identified consumer demand as their motivating force. Multiple respondents selected the "other" category offering rationales such as, "better quality," "the health and wellness of our consumers," and "little info available about where, how, and who to buy from." It is apparent from the data that most establishments did not see a contradiction between making good business decisions and supporting the local economy.

Figure 1. Retailer Reasons for Choosing to Source Food from Local Sources

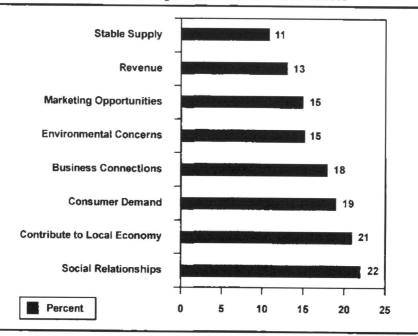

In in-depth interviews, restaurant owners and managers emphasized the importance of supporting local farmers as their main reason for purchasing local foods. They also saw these relationships as an important source of information about the availability of local food:

> The community is small so when you know somebody that buys locally they will introduce you—they will give you a name, you know? It's a lot of word of mouth. And our employees who buy at the local market will always come back to us and say, "if you're interested so-and-so has this." So it's basically word of mouth.

> She [the owner of another nearby restaurant] is always helpful in providing local people who are producing. She uses a ton of local produce, and she will always let us know, through other people that we know through her, the names of people who are producing locally.

> When we first started here all produce was bought from a produce company, and that was it, and, you know, over the years we started to meet these folks. And then we were able to buy a lot more stuff from them.

Demand for local products in Door County has been on the rise over the past few years (Figure 2). Fifty-seven percent of respondents indicated that demand for local foods had increased to some extent. Seventeen percent reported that it had increased significantly while 40 percent stated that it had increased marginally. Thirty percent reported no change. No respondents indicated a decrease in consumer demand for local products. Again, however, the primary reason for increasing purchases of local food by retailers was to support local producers.

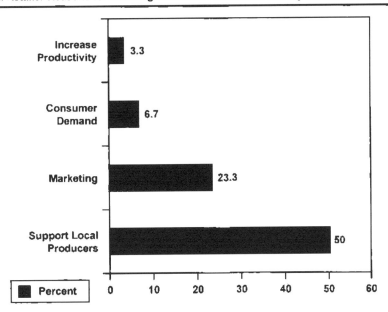

Figure 2. Retailer Reasons for Deciding to Increase Amount of Locally-Sourced Food

Although there has been a great deal of interest in local foods in the media, most restaurant managers did not report that their consumers were demanding local products. Restaurant managers discussed some of the reasons for this growth in demand for local products:

> [Buying locally is] much more personal. People are nicer to deal with, you know? When you buy something from a purveyor it is not their product; they are just doing their job, whereas these people are excited about doing it. They want you to use their product because it's theirs. The Sysco rep. doesn't care.

> The local growers understand that restaurateurs are real unhappy with corporate food, you know?

> We never serve whitefish without saying this is locally caught Lake Michigan whitefish locally caught by Door County fishermen.

> There are many local people that come here, and they go to the market as well. The more you get the name out [of the local farms from which you source], the more they can sell, which means that more they can produce as well, which is good for us because we can buy more.

Managers of restaurants and retailers ranked the severity of a variety of potential barriers to successfully bringing their yield to market locally (Figure 3). The most severe problem that agricultural producers encountered was that buyers pay too little. Small producers also struggle to match their output to the quantity requirements of local buyers.

The third obstacle is getting their products consistently and promptly to market. Finding and marketing to local buyers were not considered to be significant problems. The restaurant managers emphasized some of these same issues:

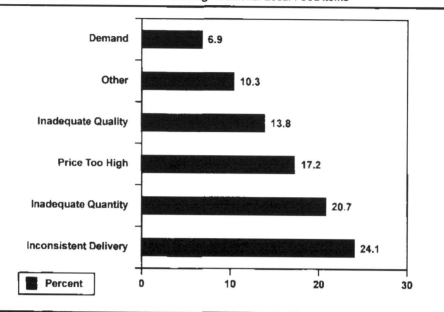

Figure 3. Retailer Reasons for Not Purchasing Additional Local Food Items

It's quantity. It really is. They just do not produce enough. I mean, we go through a lot of food, you know? In a day a lot of food, you know? I mean, we do 300 people a night during the busy season. That is the hardest thing about buying locally. So we use them [local products] a lot in the specials where you have things that you can run out of.

The delivery thing—up here I think is more of a cultural thing. Everybody is pretty laid back up here. Not many of the local farms have a consistent drive-through-town-each-day-and-drop-this-off policy. It's like, you call on Wednesday and they might say, "I have reason to be in Egg Harbor on Friday, so that's when I'll come and drop it off." And I get it. You know, they are not going to drive 20 miles to drop off some greens and spend five dollars in gas.

Direct sales are a major source of income for Door County agricultural producers. On average, Door County farms sold more to wholesalers than they did in direct sales to consumers, and restaurant/supermarket sales were, on average, quite low. The average farm had almost $30,000 in direct sales on the farm or roadside stands. At the same time, they sold about $8,000 in produce to restaurants/supermarkets, $15,000 to farmers markets, and about $92,000 to wholesalers/processors. These data suggest that there is potential for growth in the farm-to-restaurant dimension of Door County's local food network.

About one-half of the farmers reported that their sales increased at the onset of participation in local markets. In most cases, this meant selling to several more buyers and expanding their operation.

What were producers' motivations for supplying local markets? Their answers were very similar to restaurants/retailers. They were divided between self-interest and moral commitment to others in the community. The most important reason why Door County farmers sell their produce locally is the desire to contribute to the local economy. It is followed closely, however, by a desire to obtain more consistent prices for products.

Farmers were asked to rank the severity of a variety of potential barriers to successfully bringing their yield to market locally. They were most likely to identify low prices for their goods as the most significant obstacle. They also recognized that the quantity demanded by local establishments was a limitation for them. Similarly, they also tended to agree with the restaurants that consistent delivery/service could be a problem in sourcing food locally.

Implications For Culinary Tourism Beyond Door County

This case study holds lessons for other communities that wish to promote culinary tourism as a community development strategy. Nevertheless, Door County has been able to create local food linkages for culinary tourism because of its unique mix of agricultural production, natural amenities, and its robust tourism industry. Therefore, the lessons extracted from this case may not be universally applicable.

Interest in culinary tourism is growing among consumers and restaurateurs who cater to these consumers. However, there are still significant barriers to deepening the linkages of culinary tourism. These include the quality of delivery and service, the cost disconnect, and creating linkages. In Door County, there was a lack of centralized and organized means to collect and distribute local food to area food retail establishments. This limited the willingness of food retailers to source greater amounts locally. Restaurateurs were willing to increase their locally-sourced food if it were as cost-effective and simple to acquire as industrial food. Other communities that wish to promote culinary tourism might consider establishing such centralized means (such as a website) of connecting local food with local food retail, therefore improving the fit between supply and demand within the local economy.

The second barrier which other communities must overcome is the cost disconnect. Food retailers perceived that sourcing locally was more expensive than buying directly from wholesalers, but that the added cost was marginal relative to the added value of selling local food. Yet farmers consistently articulated the idea that buyers pay too little. Establishing greater communication between food producers and food vendors may help overcome this limitation in other communities. Also, educating food retailers on the added promotional opportunities that accompany culinary tourism may contribute to overcoming the price disconnect.

For culinary tourism to flourish in a community, and for the economic benefits of this sector to be distributed widely and equitably, culinary tourism must be promoted as trails rather than by individual businesses. In Door County, there were many civic associations spearheaded by the Visitor's Bureau, which organized the *Kingdom So Delicious* campaign. This program generated linkages between and within different sectors of the economy such as food vendors, art venues, agricultural producers, and retail shops. This program involved the coordinated effort of organized civil society. Therefore, in communities like Door County where civic life is robust, it may be easier to establish the linkages to successfully promote culinary tourism trails, which economically benefit a wide swath of the community.

Another consideration is that because tourism has been the leading sector of the Door County economy for several decades, there is a highly competitive restaurant market there. This market saturation has caused restaurants to cultivate niches for themselves in order to differentiate their products from those of competitors, and in many cases that niche has been local food promotion. In other, less saturated markets, it may prove more difficult to convince restaurateurs that the added value from sourcing locally justifies the costs.

Finally, Door County's proximity to several major metropolitan areas is a significant factor in its successful tourism industry generally. Door County is within 300 miles of four major cities in three states, Chicago, Minneapolis, Milwaukee, and Madison, and Door County tourism advertises in all of these markets. Therefore other communities must take advantage of their proximity to diverse urban markets to promote their culinary tourism trails.

Conclusions

Culinary tourism provides a novel approach to promoting economic development, constructing local food systems, and celebrating regional culture. It simultaneously supports the tourism and agricultural sectors and builds bridges between the two industries. Door County has been relatively successful in mobilizing its local assets as part of its tourism program.

Although culinary tourism has opened up new markets for producers, it has not had a major effect on the prices that farmers receive for their goods. The benefits would appear to be more indirect, through additional consumer spending in the region. The primary benefit to farmers may be in that it diversifies their income and protects against some of the uncertainty they may face in other markets.

There are several limitations to this study that should be noted. First, the *Kingdom So Delicious* program was developed in a region that already had an economy dominated by the tourism industry. Door County has been a major tourist destination for decades, especially for Chicago residents, and Door County has many draws. Therefore, it is difficult to measure the added economic value of culinary tourism in this setting. Additional data is needed to examine how many tourists were attracted to the region solely because of the promotion. Culinary tourism has been initiated in other regions that have not been as dependent on tourism. Evaluations of culinary tourism in these different contexts would help provide better understanding of the obstacles and opportunities this community development strategy faces.

Second, this case study does not reflect the wide variety of culinary tourism projects that exist. Additional research is needed to examine other forms of culinary tourism, such as wine tours, cooking classes, etc. These contexts may have a very different set of consequences for producers, retail establishments and others involved in culinary tourism.

This case study raises several important issues for community development and local officials interested in planning for tourism. Establishment of local markets for farmers requires some community-wide effort to coordinate supply and demand. Although a surprising number of restaurants relied on informal contacts to help them supply their needs, a more formal process would have provided some additional support in this area. Of course, intermediaries would cut into the profits of either restaurants/retail establishments or producers. One strategy might be to develop a more transparent market through a method of identifying the actual demand for and supply of food products in the region.

Second, culinary tourism typically involves collaboration across communities and different sectors of the regional economy. Regional marketing and promotion involves costs that all of the actors may bear, yet some localities may benefit more than others. Similarly, culinary tourism usually involves farmers, restaurants, retail establishments, bed and breakfast inns, and other regional businesses. How do you ensure that the various actors are rewarded fairly? There are no easy solutions for this issue. In this case study, farmers were concerned that they were not receiving a fair price for the produce. Some communities have benefited more from the promotion than others. Institutional mechanisms are needed that provide equitable solutions to these problems.

References

Allen, P. & Guthman, J. (2006). From "old school" to "farm to school:" Neoliberalization from the ground up. *Agriculture and Human Values, 23*, 401-415.

Bessiere, J. (1998). Local development and heritage: traditional food and cuisine as tourist attractions in rural areas. *Sociologia Ruralis, 38*, 21-34.

Cowell, D.K., & Green, G.P. (1994). Community attachment and spending location: The importance of place in household consumption. *Social Science Quarterly, 75*, 637-655.

Dougherty, M.L., Green, G.P., & Volenberg, D.S. (2008a). *An evaluation of food and culture tourism in door county: Retailers' perspectives on local food networks.* University of Wisconsin-Extension. Retrieved November 25, 2008 at http://www.doorcounty.org/Dean/DoorCountyRetailersReport.pdf

Dougherty, M.L., Green, G.P., & Volenberg, D.S. (2008b). *An evaluation of food and culture tourism in door county: Retailers' perspectives on local food networks.* University of Wisconsin-Extension. Retrieved November 25, 2008 at http://www.doorcounty.org/Dean/DoorCountyProducersReport.pdf

Fligstein, N. (2001). *The architecture of markets: An economic sociology of twenty-first century capital societies.* Princeton, NJ: Princeton University Press.

Granovetter, M. (1985). Economic action and social structure: the problem of embeddedness. *American Sociological Review, 91*, 481-510.

Kloppenburg, J., Lezberg, S., DeMaster, K, Stevenson, G.W., & Hendrickson, J. (2000). Tasting food, tasting sustainability: Defining the attributes of an alternative food system with competent, ordinary people. *Human Organization, 59*, 177-186.

Long, L.M. (Ed.) (2004). *Culinary tourism: Food, eating and otherness.* Lexington, KY: University of Kentucky Press.

Pirog, R. (December, 2001). Institutional local food markets. Paper presented at *From Farm to School Cafeteria: Partnerships for Supporting Farms, Improving Health, and Building Community*, Cornell University, Ithaca, New York.

Pollan, M. (2006). *The omnivore's dilemma.* New York: Penguin Books.

Reeder, R. J. & Brown, D.M. (2005). *Recreation, tourism and rural well-being.* (Economic Research Service Economic Research Report No. 7). Washington, DC: US Department of Agriculture. Retrieved May 23, 2008 at http://www.ers.usda.gov/publications/err7/err7.pdf.

Starr, A., Card, A., Benepe, C., Auld, G., Lamm, D., Smith, K. & Wilken, K. (2003). Sustaining local agriculture: Barriers and opportunities to direct marketing between farms and restaurants in Colorado. *Agriculture and Human Values, 20*, 301-321.

Telfer, D. J., & Wall, G. (1996). Linkages between tourism and food production. *Annals of Tourism Research, 23*, 635-653.

Travel Industry Association. (2007). *Comprehensive culinary travel survey provides insights on food and wine travelers.* Retrieved June 30, 2008 at http://www.tia.org/pressmedia/pressrec.asp?Item=750.

Investing in the social fabric of rural and urban communities: a comparative study of two Alabama farmers' markets

Abel Duarte Alonso[a,b] and Martin A. O'Neill[c]

[a]School of Management, University of Western Sydney, Locked Bag 1797, Penrith South DC, NSW 2751, Australia; [b]School of Marketing Tourism and Leisure, Edith Cowan University, 100 Joondalup Dr., Joondalup, 6027, Western Australia, Australia; [c]Hotel and Restaurant Management, Auburn University, 328A Spidle Hall, Auburn 36849, USA

This paper investigates the role that farmers' markets play in enhancing the social fabric of once thriving rural communities. The paper reports the findings from a comparative study of visitor motivations to two community farmers' markets in south west Alabama, one located in a rural environment and newly established, while the second, more established market (since 2004) is located in a much more populated and more affluent community. A total of 356 visitors participated in the study by completing a questionnaire. Part of the findings demonstrate that overall, visitors from both markets are more motivated to attend for the opportunity to engage in social discourse and out of a sense of support for local agriculture and farmers, than purely monetary driven exchange economics. This form of involvement, however, was more obvious among participants to the market located in the rural environment. These findings, at least with respect to the more rural respondent group, further support the contention that benefits from hosting farmers' markets are not limited to the food aspect (fresh, local foods), but communities can also significantly benefit in social terms.

Introduction

A new paradigm of social development is currently forming in some communities. The citizens of these communities "are working to construct new initiatives and civic organizations that challenge the existing food system and seek to build alternatives, in many places" (Allen, FitzSimmons, Goodman, & Warner, 2003, p. 61). In this context, the benefits of direct food buying-selling interactions between farmers and consumers, and in particular that of farmers' markets, have been recognized as tools for sustainable agriculture, sustainable development (Hinrichs, 2000, 2003; Stagl, 2004), and for rural revitalization initiatives (La Trobe, 2001). One example of these developments is that of organic produce, a market that "could contribute to a broader movement leading to collective action" (Allen & Kovach, 2000, p. 221). In fact, studies indicate that "Consumer demand may sensitize corporate agriculture to environmental and community concerns" (Alkon, 2008, p. 489), leading to the introduction of alternative (organic) products in large retail stores. At the same time, "sustainable consumption" of foods is becoming critical "as a new environmental policy objective" (Seyfang, 2006, p. 383).

Farmers' markets can make a significant contribution in this aspect, as they represent a vital link between the land, its produce and the end consumers, with particular emphasis on food freshness, the increasingly ignored yet critical face-to-face interactions, community togetherness and rural tradition. Yet, while farmers' markets have been a constant feature on the rural and urban fabric of modern United States society for some decades now, their contribution, both economically and socially remains largely under-researched (Payne, 2002). In fact, it has been argued that much of the literature tends to emphasize demographic and/or operational areas of farmers' markets (Payne, 2002). Equally important, however, is that little, if any, real consideration is given, at least from visitors' perspective, to the broader socio-economic contributions that these markets make to the sustainable fabric of host (local) and visiting participants (outsiders) and the societies within which they interact. Hunt (2007) is one of the few that explored a similar dimension, namely, visitors' interactions with vendors in Main, United States. Hunt (2007) found that such interactions contributed to visitors' expenditures at the markets. These interactions also prompted vendors to listen to consumers' demands, including regarding the use of chemicals on the fields with potentially beneficial outcomes.

In addition, very little is also known about whether the nature of the farmers' market, that is, predominantly rural or urban is a factor that determines visitors' views concerning those socio-economic aspects. For example, does the rural or urban environment where the farmers' markets are located have an impact on visitors' socio-economic needs or perceptions of such needs? Also, do visitors hold different views concerning socio-economic contributions of farmers' markets according to the environment where the farmers' market is located, that is, an economically depressed or a prosperous area? Given the dearth of knowledge on these critical dimensions, and their significant implications for communities' well-being, the present study examines the views of visitors to two seemingly different farmers' markets in the state of Alabama. One of these markets was newly established in 2009 in a rural setting of a community of approximately 9000 inhabitants with a recent industrial manufacturing past, but where the closure of its main employment source had brought economic decline. In contrast, the second market was established in 2004 and is located in an urban (over 70,000 inhabitants), more affluent area of the state of Alabama. Furthermore, the study poses several fundamental research questions to examine these areas, including the following:

- What are visitors' main motivations to visit these farmers' markets?
- What are their views with regards to their experience at these farmers' markets?
- To what extent is the social aspect, such as meeting people, important to these visitors?
- Do views of visitors to a new versus a more established farmers' market differ in their motivations to visit these places?

Respondents' answers to these questions could assist organizers of farmers' markets, as well as community, state and even national development agencies and groups to find ways to make improvements for communities, particularly those facing decline and economic hardships. Such improvements not only include encouraging citizens to consume fresh, local foods, but may also help provide an additional avenue for the public to have a forum for face-to-face interactions to connect with their social surroundings: farmers, neighbors and other fellow citizens, as well as leisure, relaxation and educational opportunities.

Literature review: the multiple beneficial aspects of farmers' markets

Described as being part of the "alternative food economy" (Winter, 2003, p. 31), farmers' markets have become a staple of the urban and rural landscape of modern day in much of the United States. The establishment of such markets has been gaining in strength at the same time that "consumer dissatisfaction with intensive farming systems and standardized farm products has grown" (Gilg & Battershill, 1998, p. 25). In fact, two opposing forces appear to be at work, with one in the form of the "global integration of the food and agricultural economy" (Campbell, 1997, p. 37), and the other through "efforts to develop local food systems attuned to the particularities of place" (p. 37). This balancing exercise is occurring at a time when there is a realization and growing concern that the globalization movement, despite its promising emphasis on bridging gaps in many areas of development, is also demonstrating to be flawed in many aspects. For example, the rapid development of food distribution channels has arguably contributed to the expansion- and influence- of large food companies while bringing many small businesses in farming communities to the brink of extinction.

The existing tension and efforts to counterbalance the rapid pace of globalization of food systems has resulted in the emergence of interest groups and different segments of consumers that have become involved in promoting the consumption of locally grown foods. On the one hand, these efforts are based on the principle that the direct producer-consumer transaction leaves out the middleman and therefore can help make this transaction more affordable for consumers (La Trobe, 2001). On the other hand, many of these stakeholders, citizens aligned with grassroots efforts to sustain local food producers are even prepared to pay more for these local products (Loureiro & Hine, 2002). This group of consumers feels a stronger moral obligation to safeguard existing small-scale, family farming. Arguably, for these individuals such ways of life represents a more sustainable agricultural approach, as opposed to prevalent farming policies that emphasize continuous growth through the more aggressive "get big or get out" business philosophy (Mascarenhas, 2001, p. 391).

Farmers' markets offer food growers the opportunity of direct access to customers; at the same time, these markets provide consumers with direct access to locally produced fresh fruits and vegetables. In some regions farmers are even "going beyond traditional marketing of fresh produce and participating in homebased microprocessing to promote value-added product" among members of their communities (Bastin, 2007, p. 91). Farmers' markets are one of the oldest forms of retailing, and have played a critical role in helping farmers gain access to consumers (Kezis, Gwebu, Peavey, & Cheng, 1998). A close, well-knit farmer-food-consumer relationship becomes critical to many communities, particularly in today's fast paced, increasingly sedentary society, for whom convenience has taken prevalence over the intrinsic aspects of food consumption. Moreover, it could be argued that aspects closely related to food consumption are increasingly being neglected, even abandoned, including relaxation, preparation of one's own food, and the socializing aspect of food consumption, aspects that for instance are still prevalent in Mediterranean cultures (Leonhäuser, Dorandt, Willmund, & Honsel, 2004). Thus, the importance of locally grown foods, and that of farmers' markets as providers of fresh produce and potential initiators of healthy lifestyles in many communities across the United States cannot be ignored.

The terms "farmers" produce market or farmers' market are used rather loosely in modern day society to describe a variety of different elements. In fact, part of the contemporary literature refers to a certain degree of confusion and vagueness as to what the term farmers' market really means:

> To identify or define a farmers' market is no easy task; for everything that is called a farmers' market may not be one, and other names are given to meetings that have the form and function of farmers' market. (Pyle, 1971, p. 167)

As far back as 1948, Wann, Cake, Elliott, and Burdette (1948) proposed that the most important criterion when defining what constitutes a farmers' market is farmers themselves selling fruits and vegetables directly to the consumer. Pyle (1971, p. 167) identifies two clear stages in the historical development of farmers' markets: (a) those that were initially set up to favor the public and then later (b) markets that were set up to protect the producers. Pyle (1971) posits that over the years a variety of terms have been used to describe farmers' markets and identifies these as the interaction of buyers, sellers and merchandise, at a fixed place and time of exchange. Pyle (1971) goes on to suggest that while the market forms in the United States have evolved in response to local needs, the market functions can be grouped under three broad headings including "economic, political and social" (p. 169).

However, more recently, other researchers have referred to farmers' markets in very practical ways, for instance, as an environment "characterized by the selling of foods and other items directly to the customer by the person who grew, reared or produced the goods" (La Trobe, 2001, p. 182). Brown's (2001, p. 670) definition is even more succinct: "Markets in which several farmers sell their own products." A more elaborated idea of farmers' markets is that these serve as a platform to satisfy "social and moral issues associated with food production" (La Trobe, 2001, p. 182). Griffin and Frongillo (2003) also refer to this social theme when they identify a variety of economic and social motivators driving farmers' participation at such markets. In fact, in their study of farmers attending upstate New York farmers' markets Griffin and Frongillo (2003) identified a number of social benefits to farmers derived from interacting with customers as well as working together with other farmer-vendors and the pride associated with marketing and the sale of their own products.

Robinson and Hartenfeld (2007, p. 3) also articulate the very real importance of the growing farmers' markets phenomenon to the social fabric of rural America and the role these markets play in bringing people of all walks of life together. The social fabric construct has been explained in several studies. For example, in referring to the work that Ahlbrant and Cunningham (1979) conducted on sense of community, McMillan and Chavis (1986) mention that those authors found that social fabric was a critical component "to commitment to neighborhood and satisfaction" (p. 7). Moreover, McMillan and Chavis (1986) suggest that Ahlbrant and Cunningham (1979) used the term social fabric "to capture the 'strengths of interpersonal relationships' as measured through different types of neighbor interactions" (p. 7). Thus, arguably social fabric refers to the strengths of relationships, including the extent or level of such strengths, between different members of a community.

In addition, buying locally has the multiplying economic benefit of re-circulating dollars throughout the local community and the wider region (Food Security Learning Center, 2009). Farmers' markets are also important as they allow the creation of a meeting place for customers and vendors to interact—an environment where customers are more likely to ask questions and receive informed answers–and offer the potential for the preserving the area's cultural identity (Food Security Learning Center, 2009). Whether in the interests of community revitalization or purely market drive economics, vendors and consumers alike are drawn to the human experience of seeing other people and sharing life experiences (O'Neil, 2005). These very human attributes are referred to as "qualities of spontaneity and sociability" (O'Neil, 2005, p. 1), both of which abound at farmers' markets.

Discussing the Davis Farmers' Market in California, Podoll (2000) explains that "Creating a network of community support and participation in the farmers' market" (p. 2) has been a central objective behind the market's establishment, with the fundamental goal to establish the market as a vital component of the local community. Of critical importance here has been harnessing a sense of local community ownership, wherein community citizens were given a voice in the market's actual development and continued growth. For example, local community groups are provided with a forum, in the form of the market, to showcase and promote their work and connect with the wider community. These events have served to cement the importance of the market within the local area and throughout the wider rural community.

Holeva (2009) addresses the issue of growing social capital through farmers' markets. Concerned with a generational decline in social interaction, this author explored the potential of urban farmers' markets as structured space designed with the intent of encouraging diverse social interactions, and therefore social capital, at the local level. Holeva's (2009) results support the major role of farmers' markets in the development of local community support networks , and addresses what Winter (2003) describes as the concept of embeddedness (Granovetter, 1985; Hinrichs, 2000; Polanyi, 1944; Sonnino, 2007), which relates to the emphasis placed on the "necessity of social relations to all economic transactions" (Winter, 2003, p. 24).

Together, all these aspects that several studies have discussed (see, for example, Agyeman, 2005; Fukuyama, 2001; Kloppenburg, Hendrickson, & Stevenson, 1996; Lyson, 2004; Putnam, 2000) have greatly contributed to the increased popularity (Alkon, 2008) and the growing number of farmers' markets being established across the nation (Brown, 2001; Govindasamy et al., 1998). At the other end, other reasons for such growth are socio-cultural aspects (Kezis et al., 1998) that include an aging population, the move towards smaller families and households and increased demand for better quality, freshness and healthy foods.

At the core of a successful market interaction are the concepts of trust and what has become known as "defensive localism" (Weir, 1994, in Allen, 1999, p. 122), in other words, the trust necessary for economic transactions to occur between local agriculture and local customers and whether, over time, such trust is founded upon earned support for local agriculture due to a discernible difference in the quality of produce purchased and consumed, or out of mere sympathy for economic circumstances. Winter (2003) states: "whether we can equate either the turn to quality or the turn to localism as the first steps towards an alternative food economy which will challenge the dominance of globalized networks and systems of provision" (p. 31). Regardless of perspective, community buy-in, identity and social interaction are as much a factor in the success of farmers' markets today as the range and freshness of the produce that is sold.

The present study investigates and compares the experiences among visitors to two different farmers markets in the state of Alabama using a quantitative approach. One of the markets is located in the City of Valley, Alabama, a city of some 9000 inhabitants (City of Valley, 2009), close to the state line between Alabama and Georgia. This town has faced severe challenges in the last few years, following the closure of two of its main employment providers, the Langdale and Riverdale Cotton Mills (City of Valley, 2009). According to those currently in charge of Langdale Mills' management and revitalization efforts, one of several strategies that the city has pursued consists of the establishment of a farmers' market; this market officially opened in the summer of 2009. One of the reasons behind this concept was to generate some movement and interest in an area that is close to the Interstate 85, around an hour's drive from Atlanta's International Airport, and that has a daily passing-by traffic of thousands of cars through one its main roads that faces the former cotton mills. Generating interest in the Langdale Mill may over time awaken interest from potential investors that see the Mill as a "dormant" opportunity with much potential. In turn, the investment on the Mill could over time create some much needed employment for locals residing in this economically depressed area.

Some 30 miles south, the Auburn University's farmers' market has been a steady feature in the university's campus since 2004 (Auburn University, 2007). Lee County, where the cities of Auburn and Opelika are located, has a population of 118,806 inhabitants (Auburn and Opelika Tourism Bureau, 2009). Both cities are physically separated by only a few miles, and combine 72,000 residents (Auburn and Opelika Tourism Bureau, 2009), including university students, staff, and many other individuals who reside in the area. These figures suggest the great potential for many visitors to venture into the university's campus to find fresh produce during the summer. Much of the produce is grown in farms scattered throughout the neighboring counties.

Methods

During the month of August 2009, both quantitative and qualitative data were collected from visitors to the farmers' markets of Langdale Mill and Auburn University. As mentioned previously, the farmers' market at Langdale Mill was introduced for the very first time in 2009, while in the case of the Auburn University the market has been ongoing for six seasons; in both cases the market is featured from late-spring through to the end of August. Of particular importance in this study was the prospect of gathering information that would allow the researchers to make comparisons between these two different environments. Fundamentally, the study sought to compare respondents of a new market located in an economically depressed area versus those participating in a more established farmers' market in a more affluent urban area.

A two-page questionnaire was developed for this study. The main reason for choosing a quantitative approach was the possibility of eliciting a sufficient number of responses within a relatively short period of time as opposed to conducting face-to-face interviews. At the same time, however, previous on-site observations identified potential time issues, particularly as in many cases visitors to farmers' markets have limited time to purchase their preferred goods, speak to the vendors or friends and have little time to complete face-to-face interviews in-situ without previous notice. Furthermore, because of potential confidentiality issues, for instance, in cases where respondents provided feedback about the market they were visiting, the approach to collect visitor information via a questionnaire was seen as more appropriate for the study. The content of the questionnaire included questions to elicit information about participants' demographic characteristics (e.g., their gender, area of residence, etc.) and their motivations for visiting the market. Appendix 1 shows an excerpt of the questionnaire and some of the areas the study examined. In this study, special emphasis is given to questions 8 and 9 as a source of respondents' responses.

Space for comments in the questionnaire also allowed respondents to provide feedback about the market. Moreover, an entire page of the questionnaire had two open-ended questions and space for comments for participants: to (a) to indicate areas of improvement, if any, that could be implemented in the farmers' market; and (b) to summarize their overall experience at the market they had visited. Thus, while half of the questionnaire was designed to collect quantitative data from visitors, the other half provided an opportunity to collect qualitative data in the form of respondents' comments.

When distributing the questionnaires, individuals visiting each market were briefly introduced to the study's objectives and invited to participate by completing the questionnaire and mailing it back to the researchers' university using a pre-paid, self-addressed envelope. This approach allowed for visitors to take the questionnaires home and complete them at their leisure, as opposed to completing the questionnaires in-situ and in the summer heat. No random questionnaire distribution was carried out; instead, to maximize responses as many visitors were approached as possible, particularly given the seasonal aspect, that is, as the farmers' market season was entering its last weeks.

A total of 572 questionnaires were distributed in both farmers' markets, 272 at Langdale Mill and 300 at the Auburn University's farmers' market. These efforts contributed to the collection of 153 usable questionnaires from Langdale Mill and 203 from the university market, a 56.3% and 67.7% response rate, respectively. Thus, 356 responses were obtained, giving an overall 62.2% response rate. The data were analyzed using the Statistical Package for the Social Sciences (SPSS), all written comments were managed and grouped into different categories using Microsoft Excel and Word. Comments from respondents from the rural farmers' market were labeled as RFM1, RFM2, etc., while comments from the urban university's market were labeled as UFM1, UFM2, etc.

Results

The data in Table 1 provide a snapshot of this study's respondents. For example, responses from female participants were three times as many as those of male participants. Furthermore, in the case of the Langdale Mill farmers' market (rural FM), 85% of the participants were from the City of Valley and the surrounding county communities. Visitors to the university farmers' market (urban FM) were even more predominantly from the city (92%). This finding suggests that the Langdale Mill market attracted groups of people who were living far from the market, and possibly far from outlets where fresh produce is available. The findings also support the view that people living in rural areas perceive the newly established farmers' market as a place to socialize and meet friends, neighbors, and/or other individuals. Moreover, as illustrated in Table 1, in general Langdale Mill respondents do not visit other farmers' markets as much as respondents from Auburn University do. As observations carried out in this study confirmed, no other near-by farmers' markets exist. Thus,

Table 1. General demographic information of visitors.

Visitors' gender	Males	%	Females	%	No answer	%	Total No.	%
Auburn University	61	30.0	141	69.5	1	0.5	203	100.0
Langdale Mill	43	28.1	109	71.2	1	0.7	153	100.0
Totals	104	29.2	250	70.2	2	0.6	356	100.0

Visitors' expenditures at the markets

Market	$1-$10	%	$11-20	%	$21+	%	No answer	%	Total No.	%
Auburn University	39	19.2	73	36.0	84	41.4	7	3.4	203	100.0
Langdale Mill	52	34.0	54	35.3	34	22.2	13	8.5	153	100.0
Totals	91	25.6	127	35.7	118	33.1	20	5.6	356	100.0

Residence	Local town/county	%	Out of country	%	No answer	%	Total No.	%
Auburn University	188	92.6	7	3.4	8	3.9	203	100.0
Langdale Mill	130	85.0	21	13.7	2	1.3	153	100.0
Totals	318	89.3	28	7.9	10	5.2	356	100.0

Whether respondents visit other farmers' markets

Market	Yes	%	No	%	No answer	%	Total No.	%
Auburn University	122	60.1	77	37.9	4	2.0	203	100.0
Langdale Mill	68	44.4	82	53.6	3	2.0	153	100.0
Totals	190	53.3	159	44.7	7	2.0	356	100.0

for the Langdale Mill respondents, having close access to a farmers' market, combined with the apparent difficulty of travelling to other markets near their rural environment may be of special significance. This aspect is particularly true regarding the opportunity to meet other individuals and reinforce existing personal and other social ties. Regarding the expenditure that each group incurred during their visit, it became clear that respondents at the university farmers' market appeared to be the more affluent group, or at least were inclined to spend more during their visit ($\chi^2_{(2,\ n=336)} = 17.026$, ($p = 0.000$)).

Asked about the extent to which meeting other people was an important reason for them to visit the market, Table 2 illustrates that a much higher percentage of responses (41.2% versus 20.7%) from visitors to the Langdale Mill farmers' market (Rural FM) clearly identified the importance of this element as a motivator of their farmers' market experience. When potential differences between the rural (m = 3.22) and university markets (m = 2.40) and visitors' views on "meeting people" as a strong reason for visiting the markets were compared, a statistically significant relationship ($p < 0.001$) was noticed. The view that many visitors to the rural market place much importance on strengthening the social fabric of their community is also identified in many comments made in the space provided in the questionnaire. For example, five participants acknowledged the opportunity to meet other people, with some of them vying to continue to return and use the market as a meeting place:

RFM1: A lovely time to share with others, meet friends and enjoy eating all the beautiful vegetables, flowers, and canned things plus fruits. Look forward to the market each week. Please do this again next year.

Table 2. Selected differences between the two groups of visitors.

Scales	Rural FM (n)	Rural FM (%)	Urban FM (n)	Urban FM (%)	Totals (n)	Totals (%)
Importance of meeting other people at the farmers' market (I can meet other people)						
Unimportant to very unimportant	44	28.8	103	50.7	147	41.3
Neither important nor unimportant	36	23.5	48	23.6	84	23.6
Important to very important	63	41.2	42	20.7	105	29.5
Did not answer	10	6.5	10	4.9	20	5.6
Totals	153	100.0	203	100.0	356	100.0
I can meet other people	Urban	193	2.40	1.370	.000**	
	Rural	143	3.22	1.470		
Importance of meeting local/state farmers at the farmers' market (I can meet local/state farmers)						
Unimportant to very unimportant	23	15.0	47	23.2	70	19.7
Neither important nor unimportant	31	20.3	52	25.6	83	23.3
Important to very important	89	58.2	99	48.8	188	52.8
Did not answer	10	6.5	5	2.5	15	4.2
Totals	153	100.0	203	100.0	356	100.0
I can meet local/state farmers	Urban	198	3.38	1.319	.007**	
	Rural	143	3.78	1.329		

Notes: Independent t-tests. **Statistically significant.

RFM2: It's a good place to meet friends.
RFM3: Enjoy seeing friends and neighbors.
RFM4: It was a pleasant experience, meeting friends and also making friends with some of the vendors.
RFM5: Visited with friends and relatives I have not seen in a while... Much more enjoyable than seeing them in Wal-Mart, the ultimate conformist locations. I will return every week when possible.

I take my 87 year old grandmother every Friday to Valley. It is fun for her to get out and it is a great way for us to spend time together.
RFM8: Everyone (farmers, staff and visitors) seemed to be happy and having fun. It became a great gathering place for friends.
RFM9: Loved meeting farmers and visit neighbors; people were so friendly.
RFM10: We love meeting new friends and helping to support our farmers.

Responses were also very demonstrative towards the farmers selling their produce at the market. The opportunity to buy fresh produce and interact with the food growers also demonstrated participants' interest in connecting with the land. In fact, a statistically significant difference was identified ($p < 0.007$) when respondents' views between the rural (mean = 3.78) and the university market (mean = 3.38) were compared with regards to meeting the farmers as a reason for visiting the markets. In addition, people's need to have both a tangible and intangible experience of the senses, that is, touching and smelling the produce, or discussing aspects of agriculture with the food growers was manifested in their responses. Such a need might be very strong among many respondents, particularly as lifestyle issues, for instance, living far from rural communities, or the absence of public events (e.g., a farmers' market) in their surroundings may have had negative impacts on these citizens, who consequently become disenfranchised from social groups or the local community:

RFM6: My husband and I visited our local farmers' market each week but two since they started it. We enjoyed seeing folks we know and talking with the vendors. We are going to miss this when they close the end of the month. Can't wait till next year.
RFM7: Really enjoyed meeting the farmers... they have become friends.

These comments are in line with studies referring to farmers' markets as places of gathering for the local community, as well as a source of many different fresh foods, flowers and crafts (see, for example, Hunt, 2007; O'Neil, 2005; Podoll, 2000; Robinson & Hartenfeld, 2007). In the cases above, the farmers' market clearly evokes pleasant images of meeting other individuals and socializing. For another group of participants, food-related motives, such as having an opportunity to find an after-sought food item seem to be almost as equally important to them as the social aspect of the market:

RFM11: I would not otherwise be able to purchase Chilton County peaches in local area.
RFM12: It would be nice for you to circulate contact info on the vendors so that we may continue to support them in the off season (Amish bread is seasonless, right?!).
RFM13: It was great to be able to buy fresh bread, honey, etc. from local artisans.

A different respondent evoked childhood memories that had a clear impact on his motivation to participate in the market and support local food growers (**RFM14**): "I am happy to support local and state farmers. I appreciate their hard work—having grown up on a farm myself. I enjoy the fresh produce and I also enjoy meeting new people and seeing old friends as I shop." Other participants acknowledged changes to their diet and how these were intrinsically related to their visitation to the farmers' market (**RFM15**): "We change our eating ways from eating unhealthy foods and starting eating fruit instead of junk food. Myself and my kids love peaches, apples, grapes, oranges, bananas, pears, pineapple." A different visitor echoed the wish of many other respondents that the market should continue past the summer months (**RFM16**): "The farmers' market is a positive addition to Valley. We need more farmers to sell their goods for competitive prices. It would be nice, if possible, to have vendors sell apples, pumpkins, and other fall items during the fall season."

The university's market

As compared to the City of Valley's visitor group, only one fifth (42, 20.7%) of the visitors to the farmers' market taking place at the university's campus considered meeting friends important. Despite the lower percentage of responses, there were comments suggesting that visitors' interaction with farmers, the local community, or even spending time with family members were high points in their visit, including the following:

> **UFM1**: I like meeting people at the market and have enjoyed the times we have gone this year.
> **UFM2**: I enjoy the market overall. I talk to different people about how they cook different vegetables and make desserts with fruit. I see old friends and old work mates.
> **UFM3**: I really enjoy the experience of meeting with the growers and interaction with other buyers. There is such a variety of fresh produce, plants, etc. It is great to know that my vegetables didn't travel hundreds of miles to reach me and that they are so fresh and have not been placed on cold storage.
> **UFM4**: We enjoyed our visit. My son liked playing in the grassy area in the center while I shopped.

While the links between the "social capital" and the farmers' market were much less accentuated in comments of those participants to the urban market, there were also instances demonstrating visitors' value of other very positive human aspects, including trust. Arguably, this element is more prevalent in predominantly small rural communities, where people tend to know each other, and where traditions play a critical role in everyday social interactions, to the point where honesty is highly regarded, and possibly interpreted in a different, much more serious way. Hinrichs (2000) notes that "Activists and academic analysts often assume that trust and social connection characterize direct agricultural markets..." (p. 295). For some respondents, their experience at the market became a reminder of traditional values that, like trust still prevail in many rural communities, where the (slower) pace of life allows for a different form of reflecting about and interpreting life:

> **UFM14**: On August 14th I forgot a bag filled with yellow squash and green peppers not realizing until after the market closed. When returning the following week August 21 I stopped at the vendor where it was left and the man remembered saying it was home in his refrigerator. Since he didn't carry green peppers but did yellow squash he was very kind in giving me yellow squash in replacement. Kindness in Auburn market will be shared with others and I shall return to this vendor for his kindness and honesty.

For many other participants, the value of finding fresh and/or different varieties of local produce was equally as important. These visitors' comments suggest that they have developed a sense and a preference for the "locality" aspect of foods they purchase. In addition, these visitors are inclined to favor alternative, low-scale farming systems as opposed to those more intensive and standardized that have led to growing consumer dissatisfaction (Gilg & Battershill, 1998):

> **UFM5**: I like the variety of fresh produce, flowers, baked goods, soap, and such. There is a great community atmosphere. I look forward to it every year. I appreciate the opportunity to buy local. I think it is important to do so—in terms of support for agriculture, economic impact and community strength.
> **UFM6**: Going to the farmers' market is so much more fun, personal and rewarding than going to a grocery chain.
> **UFM7**: Having grown up on a farm, I have always enjoyed farmers' markets, roadside fruit stands, etc. It's nice to be reminded of years gone by in addition to being able to get fresh produce.
> **UFM8**: I like the idea that you can buy fresh baked goods as well as fresh produce. It is fun to go there and I feel good about what I am feeding my family as well as supporting our local farmers.
> **UFM9**: I love being able to buy local produce at the market. I like knowing where the food I eat comes from and supporting local farmers ... The produce is always fresh, and I know what I am eating is nutritional and environmentally—friendly.
> **UFM10**: I really enjoy buying my corn from here. It's some of the best corn I have purchased this year ... I also love the fruit at the market. The fruit is much fresher than from the grocery story ... It's great to shop here instead of the grocery market.

Evidence of positive outcomes through educational initiatives at farmers' markets has been reflected in the contemporary literature (see, for example, Anderson et al., 2001; Feenstra, 1997), particularly with regards to an increase in fruit and vegetable consumption patterns. Similarly, in this study the importance of the educational experience, both in terms of learning about the products and also in nutritional terms was also reflected in respondents' comments:

> **UFM11**: We both (husband and wife) love to come here because of the quality, nutritional content and because it is here on a dependable schedule. Please keep making this available to the ... community. It is one of the many things that make the quality of life here so great!
> **UFM12**: ... this [farmers' market] one is my favorite. The vendors tend to be more knowledgeable and diverse ...
> **UFM13**: Very pleasant experience each year. For the most part, vendors and shoppers are friendly and polite. Most vendors are willing/eager to answer questions about their products.

In line with previous reports that refer to the importance of freshness in conjunction with the opportunity to have direct contact with farmers as two of the main reasons for visiting farmers' markets (Govindasamy et al., 1998), several respondents also commented on freshness and taste of the foods they purchased:

> **UFM16**: My overall experience of the market has been a very positive one. I love all the fresh fruit and vegetables, grains, honey, etc. I come almost every week and glad it's been extended a couple of weeks ... at least it seems so! Thank you for holding it each year.
> **UFM17**: We have enjoyed the fruits and vegetables that were purchased at the market.
> **UFM18**: I am glad that we have the opportunity to buy fresh local produce to support local farmers.
> **UFM19**: A very positive experience. I

thought fresh, delicious produce and met the people that grew it—all at a great price.

Other studies, however, identify an "ongoing social interaction between producers and consumers;" in turn, this interaction serves the purpose of a "more individualized and locally contingent quality evaluation" (Kirwan, 2006, p. 310). A final area identified in respondents' comments suggests that some producers are exploring the organic side of food growing, and there are consumers interested in and receptive to these produce.

> **UFM20**: I was pleased to see organic produce added at the end of the season and eggs also.
> **UFM21**: I enjoy talking to the vendors. I learn something new every time I go and enjoy the atmosphere. I like that there are organic grains and also baked goods. I enjoy the late afternoon time.

These comments seem to be in line with Alkon (2008), who explains that those advocating "environmental sustainability and social justice increasingly pursue their goals through the promotion of so-called "green" products such as locally grown organic produce" (p. 487).

Summary and conclusions

This study examined visitors' experiences at two seemingly distinct farmers' markets, one recently established in an economically depressed rural area, while the second, located in an urban area populated with close to 100,000 people, has been running for six years. Clearly, and as it is common in many other environments and referred to in studies (see, for example, Archer, Sánchez, Vignali, & Chaillot, 2003; Onianwa, Mojica, & Wheelock, 2006) the aspect of having weekly access to fresh, local produce is one of the main reasons among participants to visit farmers' markets. However, there is very little discussion in the contemporary community development related literature regarding the contribution of farmers' markets in environments that while physically or geographically close, may differ in socio-economic terms. In this context, the present study expands from the literature and adds new insights on the farmers' market-local community dimension.

For example, while some differences were noted concerning the reasons for visiting the market between both markets, overall, both groups of respondents share very similar views concerning the intrinsic (social) value the farmers' market represents to them. That said, the rural environment of the new farmers' market in the City of Valley seems to have an even more special value for participants, as some 40% respondents in this town considered meeting people as critical for visiting the farmers' market important of their choice. Such outcome, together with many comments wishing for the extension of the market after its conclusion at the end of the summer of 2009, or at least hoping for the market to be open again in 2010 underlines the value that many people in rural areas, in this specific case in an economically depressed area, place in either re-creating, maintaining or strengthening the social fabric of their community. Thus at least in this regard the study's findings have several implications for farmers' market stakeholders and for society in general. First, however, there is a need to provide some context and argument supporting these implications.

Today's inexorable push for globalization has had a number of impacts for many businesses, particularly for small food growers who face a number of unfair challenges. For example, the threat of cheaper food imports, or that of distribution channels that, while arguably more affordable and convenient for millions of consumers, highlight the plight of "food miles" and other unsustainable food systems have had a very negative impact on small food producers. Not surprisingly, small farmers' very survival is at stake (Starr et al., 2003); despite this gloomy scenario, researchers argue that "globalizing trends in food systems are likely to continue ..." (Pretty, Ball, Lang, & Morison, 2005, p. 16).The benefits for urban areas in the form of fast and constant food supplies, often of unknown origin have also given way to many issues that are affecting society in many regards. For instance, while many years ago civilization had a direct relationship with the land and its produce, recent decades have witnessed an ever increasing psychological gap between urban and rural areas.

In this new world order people's attachment with the land has all but disappeared for millions of citizens, whose life style and daily needs have alienated them from the land. These developments have also affected "modern" societies such as that of the United States, and the notion of "going back to basics" seems more distant than ever. Not surprisingly, one important area of concern in the United States agricultural sector is that of "the socioeconomic sustainability of rural communities and family farms" (Brodt, Feenstra, Kozloff, Klonsky, & Tourte, 2006, p. 75). In this context, Brodt et al. (2006) furthermore state that "... sustainable farming practices tend to require more locally produced inputs, to replace agrochemicals obtained in distant markets, and so they will increase local trade and support businesses within communities" (p. 76). Awareness of the socioeconomic aspects of farming communities demonstrates that despite these negative realities, efforts, if at the very least symbolic, are being made to slow the rapid pace of globalization and large-scale farming and distribution systems that many argue cannot be sustained in the long-term.

Grass-root type consumer groups who long the "old days" and vie to support traditional "mom and pop" farming businesses, together with other consumers who seek freshness—even more affordable food prices—represent two groups whose level of involvement in establishing strong and sustainable farmer-consumer transactions has increased. These two groups are growing, not only as part of a "pacifist" rebellion against the monotony and large food corporations, but also to alert society about forthcoming challenges. Moreover, these groups are seeking to preserve what is left of traditionally rural ways, as well as to increase awareness and appreciation for the land and for those whose effort and sweat contribute towards rural communities' preservation of their social fabric and farming traditions. An extension of grower-consumer relationships is illustrated in farmers' market environments, where food growers showcase their produce, seek to educate consumers, or simply engage in conversations that contribute to the critical social interaction aspect that has all but disappeared in the more rigid and impersonal supermarket chain environments. Finally, today's emphasis in many consumer environments concerning the availability of local foods (Ostrom, 2006) or the promotion of healthier eating habits (Flora & Gillespie, 2009) further emphasize the strategic role of farmers' markets in promoting community development in different ways.

Several limitations are recognized in this study. For example, while the number of respondents seems appropriate for an exploratory study of this caliber, an even larger number at each market and during the entire summer season might have provided a more robust group of respondents and consequently of more data that would have helped to identify important insights about visitors. Also, while many respondents provided very illustrative comments about their experience, conducting face-to-face interviews could have enhanced the quality of the collected data in several regards. Moreover, interviews might have provided many respondents with an opportunity to further elaborate on their hand-written comments. In addition, seeking a dialogue directly with participants via a face-to-face conversation might have also contributed to identifying reasons among those who did not comment on their experience. Despite these limitations, this study provides an initial examination about a topic that has enormous interest from different angles, including rural sustainability, the importance of farmers-consumers relationships, differences in perception between visitors to rural-based as opposed to urban-based farmers' markets, and also the value that visitors place on the social aspect of famers' market visitation.

The overall findings also suggest several avenues for future research. One such area of subsequent investigation could be studying whether other surrounding rural areas of the sites chosen in this study consider the establishment of farmers' markets and seek similar benefits as the participating farmers' markets, other communities in Alabama or elsewhere in the United States. The long physical distance from one town to the next is clearly a challenge for many citizens, as well as the time, effort and cost of visiting farmers' markets physically distant from their homes. An additional area of future research could be undertaken with regard to the benefits that farmers' markets have in communities that, like those of larger urban areas, have existed for many years. Future research could also examine the progression of the participating markets in this study, particularly with regards to further enhancement of what is currently on offer in these markets for the benefit of the local communities. At the same time, the findings of such studies could contribute to alerting rural and government bodies of the critical importance of making strides to improve rural communities' livelihood, including through concerted efforts to maintain farmer-consumer links alive.

References

Agyeman, J. (2005). *Sustainable communities and the challenge of environmental justice.* New York: New York University Press.

Ahlbrant, R.S., & Cunningham, J.V. (1979). *A new public policy for neighbourhood preservation.* New York: Praeger.

Alkon, A.H. (2008). From value to values: Sustainable consumption at farmers markets. *Agriculture and Human Values, 25,* 487–498.

Allen, P. (1999). Reweaving the food security safety net: Mediating entitlement and entrepreneurship. *Agriculture and Human Values, 16,* 117–129.

Allen, P., FitzSimmons, M., Goodman, M., & Warner, K. (2003). Shifting plates in the agrifood landscape: The tectonics of alternative agrifood initiatives in California. *Journal of Rural Studies, 19,* 61–75.

Allen, P., & Kovach, M. (2000). The capitalist composition of organic: The potential of markets in fulfilling the promise of organic agriculture. *Agriculture and Human Values, 17,* 221–232.

Anderson, J.V., Bybee, D.I., Brown, R.M., McLean, D.F., Garcia, E.M., Breer, M.L., & Schillo, B.A. (2001). 5 a day fruit and vegetable intervention improves consumption in a low income population. *Journal of the American Dietetic Association, 101*(2), 195–202.

Archer, G.P., Sánchez, J.G., Vignali, G., & Chaillot, A. (2003). Latent consumers' attitude to farmers' markets in North West England. *British Food Journal, 105,* 487–497.

Auburn and Opelika Tourism Bureau. (2009). *Travel and transportation.* Retrieved November 3, 2009, from http://www.aotourism.com/travel/frmTravel.aspx

Auburn University. (2007). *AU famers' market kicking off 2007 season.* Retrieved November 20, 2009, from http://www.ag.auburn.edu/adm/comm/news/2007/farmers_market_kickoff.php

Bastin, S. (2007). Options for the economic health of farmers, farmers markets and communities: Homebased fruit and vegetable microprocessing. *Community Development: Journal of the Community Development Society, 38*(8), 91–99.

Brodt, S., Feenstra, G., Kozloff, R., Klonsky, K., & Tourte, L. (2006). Farmer-community connections and the future of ecological agriculture in California. *Agriculture and Human Values, 23,* 75–88.

Brown, A. (2001). Counting farmers markets. *Geographical Review, 91*(4), 655–674.

Campbell, D. (1997). Community-controlled economic development as a strategic vision for the sustainable agriculture movement. *Making Waves, 12,* 37–44.

City of Valley. (2009). *Visitors.* Retrieved July 2, 2009, from http://www.cityofvalley.com/home/visitors

Feenstra, G.W. (1997). Local food systems and sustainable communities. *American Journal of Alternative Agriculture, 12*(1), 28–36.

Flora, C.B., & Gillespie, A.H. (2009). Making healthy choices to reduce childhood obesity: Community capitals and food and fitness. *Community Development, 40,* 114–122.

Food Security Learning Center. (2009). *Farmers' markets – Introduction.* Retrieved October 25, 2009, from http://www.whyhunger.org/programs/fslc/topics/farmersa-market.html

Fukuyama, F. (2002). Social capital and development: The coming agenda. *SAIS Review, 12*(1), 23–37.

Gilg, A.W., & Battershill, M. (1998). Quality farm food in Europe: a possible alternative to the industrialised food market and to current agro-environmental policies: Lesson from France. *Food Policy, 23*(1), 24–40.

Govindasamy, R., Zurbriggen, M., Italia, J., Adelaja, A., Nitzsche, P., & VanVranken, R. (1998). Farmers markets: consumer trends, preferences, and characteristics. New Jersey Agricultural Experiment Station. P-02137-7-98.

Granovetter, M. (1985). Economic action and social structure: The problem of embeddedness. *American Journal of Sociology, 91,* 481–510.

Griffin, M.R., & Frongillo, E.A. (2003). Experiences and perspectives of farmers from upstate New York farmers' markets. *Agriculture and Human Values, 20,* 189–203.

Hinrichs, C.C. (2000). Embeddedness and local food systems: Notes on two types of direct agricultural market. *Journal of Rural Studies, 16*(3), 295–303.

Hinrichs, C.C. (2003). The practice and politics of food system localization. *Journal of Rural Studies, 19,* 33–45.

Holeva, P.D. (2009). *Growing social capital: Investigating the relationship between farmers' markets and the development of social support networks in Ann Arbor.* (Unpublished Master's thesis). Department of Geography, Miami University, Oxford, Ohio. Retrieved October 17, 2009, from http://etd.ohiolink.edu/send-pdf.cgi/Holeva%20Paul%20D.pdf?acc_num=miami1247776009

Hunt, A. (2007). Consumer interactions and influences on farmers' markets vendors. *Renewable Agriculture and Food Systems, 22,* 54–66.

Kezis, A., Gwebu, T., Peavey, S., & Cheng, H-T. (1998). A study of consumers at a small farmers' market in Maine: Results from a 1995 survey. *Journal of Food Distribution Research, 29*(1), 91–99.

Kirwan, J. (2006). The interpersonal world of direct marketing: Examining conventions of quality at UK farmers' markets. *Journal of Rural Studies, 22,* 301–312.

Kloppenburg, J., Jr., Hendrickson, J., & Stevenson, G.W. (1996). Coming into the foodshed. *Agriculture and Human Values, 13,* 33–42.

La Trobe, H. (2001). Farmers' markets: Consuming local rural produce. *International Journal of Consumer Studies, 25*(3), 181–192.

Leonhäuser, I-U., Dorandt, S., Willmund, E., & Honsel, J. (2004). The benefit of the Mediterranean diet – Considerations to modify German food patterns. *European Journal of Nutrition, 43*(1), 31–38.

Loureiro, M.L., & Hine, S. (2002). Discovering niche markets: A comparison of consumer willingness to pay for local (Colorado grown), organic, and GMO-free products. *Journal of Agricultural and Applied Economics, 34*(3), 477–487.

Lyson, T. (2004). *Civic agriculture: Reconnecting farm, food, and community.* Boston: Tufts University Press.

Mascarenhas, M. (2001). Farming systems research: Flexible diversification of a small family farm in southeast Michigan. *Agriculture and Human Values, 18,* 391–401.

McMillan, D.W., & Chavis, D.M. (1986). Sense of community: A definition and theory. *Journal of Community Psychology, 14,* 6–23.

O'Neil, D. (2005). *Making places.* Retrieved August 20, 2009, from http://www.pps.org/markets/info/markets_articles/ten_characteristics

Onianwa, O., Mojica, M., & Wheelock, G. (2006). Consumer characteristics and views regarding farmers markets: An examination of on-site survey data of Alabama consumers. *Journal of Food Distribution Research, 37,* 119–125.

Ostrom, M. (2006). Everyday meanings of "local food": Views from home and field. *Community Development, 37,* 65–78.

Payne, T. (2002). *US farmers' markets 2000: A study of emerging trends* (pp. 1–40). Retrieved October 21 2009 from http://agmarketing.extension.psu.edu/ComFarmMkt/PDFs/emerg_trend_frm_mrkt.pdf

Podoll, H. (2000). *A case study of The Davis Farmers' Market; connecting farms and community.* Retrieved October 6 2009 from http://www.sarep.ucdavis.edu/cdpp/Davis.htm

Polanyi, K. (1944). *The great transformation: The political and economic origins of our time.* New York: Rineheart and Co.

Pretty, J.N., Ball, A.S., Lang, T., & Morison, J.I.L. (2005). Farm costs and food miles: An assessment of the full cost of the UK weekly food basket. *Food Policy, 30,* 1–19.

Putnam, R.D. 2000. *Bowling alone: The collapse and revival of American community.* New York: Simon and Schuster.

Pyle, J. (1971). Farmers' markets in the United States: functional anachronisms? *Geographical Review, 61*(2), 167–197.

Robinson, J.M., & Hartenfeld, J.A. (2007). *The farmers' market book.* Bloomington, Indiana: Indiana University Press.

Seyfang, G. (2006). Ecological citizenship and sustainable consumption: Examining local organic food networks. *Journal of Rural Studies, 22*(4), 383–395.

Sonnino, R. (2007). Embeddedness in action: Saffron and the making of the local in southern Tuscany. *Agriculture and Human Values, 24,* 61–74.

Stagl, S. (2004). Local organic food markets: Potentials and limitations for contributing to sustainable development. *Empirica, 23*(2), 145–162.

Starr, A., Card, A., Benepe, C., Auld, G., Lamm, D., Smith, K., & Wilken, K. (2003). Sustaining local agriculture: Barriers and opportunities to direct marketing between farms and restaurants in Colorado. *Agriculture and Human Values, 20,* 301–321.

Wann, J.L., Cake, E.W., Elliott, W.H., & Burdette, R.F. (1948). *Farmers' produce markets in the United States. Part 1, History and description.* Marketing research report No. 17, Washington, DC: US Department of Agriculture, Farm Credit Administration.

Weir, M. (1994). Urban poverty and defensive localism. *Dissent,* 337–342.

Winter, M. (2003). Embeddedness, the new food economy and defensive localism. *Journal of Rural Studies, 19,* 23–32.

Appendix 1. Excerpt of the questionnaire tool

1) How often do you visit farmers' markets? Daily O   Weekly O   Monthly O
2) Apart from your 'regular' farmers' market, do you travel to others? Yes O   No O
3) What was your approximate expenditure at the market today?
4) Your gender is … Male O   Female O
5) Your age group is …
   20 years old and below O   21–35 O   36–50 O   51–65 O   66 and above O
6) In which county do you reside?
7) How important are the following reasons for visiting farmers' markets in general? Please circle

I can meet other people	1	2	3	4	5
I can buy fresh produce	1	2	3	4	5
I can meet local/state farmers	1	2	3	4	5
I can learn about the products I purchase	1	2	3	4	5
I can help support local/state producers	1	2	3	4	5
I can support the local/state economy	1	2	3	4	5
Market location	1	2	3	4	5
I can get answers about the produces nutritional value from farmers	1	2	3	4	5
I can get answers about how the foods are grown from farmers	1	2	3	4	5

Other reasons:

8) Please let us know what, if anything, you would like to change about the market.
9) Please tell us about your overall experience so that we can work towards continually improving the range of products on offer and service you receive:

"Growing Wellness": The Possibility of Promoting Collective Wellness through Community Garden Education Programs

Michelle L. D'Abundo and Andrea M. Carden

The Community Garden Education Program was created as a way to combat obesity in a low-income eastern North Carolina community. Observations were conducted throughout and two focus groups were held at the end of the first phase of the program to reveal the participants' perspectives. Focus group findings indicated that the initial program goals of administrators focused on obesity reduction were different from participant goals that focused on wellness and community development. In addition, participants reported improved food sustainability as a result of the Community Garden Education Program. The implications of this research include suggestions for promoting Community Food Sustainability (CFS) that may lead to collective wellness.

According to the 2005 North Carolina Behavioral Risk Factor Surveillance System (NC BRFSS), 60% of adults of the overall population were overweight or obese in New Hanover County. The situation for African Americans living in New Hanover County was more serious with a reported 73% of the population being overweight or obese. Such high rates of obesity seriously impact the mental and physical well being of individuals and communities. As part of Cape Fear Healthy Carolinians Obesity Prevention Initiative (OPI), the Community Garden Education Program was a collaborative effort, with the local housing authority and the local university, focused on reducing obesity rates in the community. While the original conception of the Community Garden Education Program was focused on obesity reduction through education about nutrition and gardening, other goals emerged from the participant experiences that focused on wellness and community development.

Literature Review

Research has shown numerous benefits of community gardening. Brown and Jameton (2000) outlined the public health benefits of urban agriculture as providing food security, personal wellness, community betterment, and environmental health. According to Armstrong (2000), benefits of community gardens include improvement of local, sustainable food systems; improvement of job skills and employment opportunities; addressing problems of depression and other mental health issues; addressing the need of green spaces and appearance; and decreased crime in urban neighborhoods. Hanna and Oh (2000) identified community gardens as a way to help alleviate poverty in urban communities by providing fresh produce, value formation, neighborhood improvement, while developing a sense of community and satisfying labor.

Community gardens can play a role in the development of a community. Relf as cited in Malakoff (1995) says that plants and greening activities can lead to community development in three ways: provide a more livable physical environment through control of temperature, noise and pollution; create a positive community image and collaborative opportunities for residents. In particular, community gardens may facilitate improved social networks and organizational capacity in the communities in lower income and minority neighborhoods.

Gardening provides opportunities for everyone involved to develop skills in leadership, community organizing, cultural competency, program planning, implementation, and evaluation. Community improvement resulting from gardening efforts can range from knowledge and skill enhancement to behavioral and systems change (Twiss et. al, 2003). Community gardens may also foster neighborhood organizing and provide a physical location for residents to meet each other; to socialize, to learn about other organizations, activities, and issues in their local community (Armstrong, 2000). According to Schukoske (2000), "Gardening has developed as a viable alternative to vacancy, and has often led to increased safety, beautification, and cooperation within the community" (p. 361-2).

The concept of wellness has been used to describe the holistic health of individuals and is increasingly being used to discuss the well being of communities as a whole. In this research, the concept of wellness is used not only to describe individual well being, but also details how a community garden education program can affect the wellness of a community. The definition of wellness used in this study is "a multidimensional state of being describing the existence of positive health in an individual as exemplified by quality of life and a sense of well being" (Corbin & Pangrazi, 2001, p. 1). From this perspective, the term wellness is used as a positive component of health where the concept of positive health refers to well being and quality of life.

In health education and health promotion, the sub-dimensions of wellness usually include physical, social, intellectual, emotional (mental), and spiritual. In community psychology, the concept of community wellness has been theorized in different ways. Totikidis and Prilleltensky (2006) propose a community wellness model that identifies well being on three levels: personal, relational, and collective. Personal well being includes intrapersonal factors like physical health, love, competence, and self-esteem. Relational well being includes interpersonal factors like social support, affection, belonging, collaboration, respect for diversity, and democratic participation. Collective well being includes economic security, social justice, adequate health and social services, low crime, adequate infrastructure, and a clean environment.

The concept of community wellness has been used to guide research in many settings with diverse populations. Prilleltensky and Fox (2007) explored how wellness is achieved by balancing personal, relational, and collective needs as they relate to justice. These concepts have been applied to the topics of children and families (Prilleltensky & Nelson,

2000), youth and democracy (Evans & Prilleltensky, 2007), and social action with youth (Morsillo & Prilleltensky, 2007).

Cadell, Karabanow, and Sanchez (2001) propose a cyclical model of wellness that focuses on community-building through reliance and empowerment. At the individual level, these concepts build personal strength, courage, and vision. At the community level, the concepts represent belonging, suggest a coping ability, and promote advocacy.

In this research, we propose ways to enrich dimensions of wellness in gardening programs while also exploring the possibility of a community concept of wellness that refers to how quality of life, a sense of well being, and the dimensions of wellness can be promoted in a community of people. Although this was not our original intention, the concept of wellness emerged as the guiding theoretical perspective of the research.

The purpose of this research was to explore the perspectives of participants from the Community Garden Education Program by applying a community wellness perspective. While obesity prevention was the initial goal of program administrators, the program participants noted various aspects of wellness and community development as outcomes of the program. The description below provides a summary of activities provided to participants during the program.

Methodology

Community garden education program

The Community Garden Education Program was a collaborative effort with the local housing authority and the local university that aimed to reduce obesity rates through classes focused on nutrition and gardening. A summary of the Community Garden Education Program activities from the beginning to the conclusion of the first funding cycle is included. First, a representative of the local housing authority approached community members about their existing gardens. A male in the adult focus group, Jack, was hesitant at first because he thought he was going "to get in trouble" for planting on city property. However, the representative was interested in starting a community garden. After much planning and meetings with the local housing authority, the university, and pubic housing residents, a small amount of funding was secured to implement the Community Garden Education Program.

The representative from the local housing authority donated land for the project that was located about 20 miles away from the public housing community. However, many participants do not attend trips to the community garden so the housing authority representative explored the option of conducting the garden on the public housing site. Meanwhile, participants that already had gardens continued to grow their own gardens outside of their residences.

As part of the Community Garden Education Program, classes were offered to participants about nutrition, cooking, and gardening. Classes in October 2006 focused on gardening education for participants. Three classes in November 2007 focused on education concerning nutritional food preparation and diet.

On October 19, 2006, the Community Garden Education Program Kick-Off event was held with participants completing demographic and a pre-program survey. A representative of the local Cooperative Extension gave a presentation on vegetable gardening. Participants showed enthusiasm about starting a community garden at the public housing complex and asked many questions about the project. There were 15– 25 participants in attendance. Based on the observations of an OPI representative, the older adults were more engaged than the young adults.

On October 30, 2006, the same representative of the local Cooperative Extension gave a presentation at the garden site that focused on soil sampling. Participants asked questions and made suggestions throughout the presentation. Participants received handouts that provided instructions for planting crops. There were 10 adults and 11 younger adults in attendance.

On November 14, 2006, a representative of the local Cooperative Extension gave a presentation that focused on healthy eating, food handling, and dietary guidelines.

Of the 11 total participants, 7 participants were under the age of 18. Several participants shared their dietary habits with the group and again older adults were more focused than younger adults.

On November 21, 2006, a presentation by the same cooperative extension representative held at the Cooperative Extension office kitchen focused on preparing healthy foods. There were 8 participants including 6 youth and 2 adults. Participants responded to requests for interaction and agreed to assist presenter when asked. There seemed to be general enthusiasm among participants.

On December 2006, a post-program celebration was held. Participants completed post-tests and participated in focus groups. Participants were presented with certificates of presentation and healthy foods and drink were provided.

Participants

In total, 35 families participated in Community Garden Education Program activities from several public housing sites and in the local neighborhood. The focus group participants consisted of people that attended the post program celebration. Focus groups were held separately with young adults and adults. In the young adults groups, six African Americans ages 14–30 participated with one male and five females. On average, the young adults that participated in the focus groups attended three of the Community Garden Education Program functions.

Table 1.

Name	Age	Race	Description
Brandy	54	African American	Doer, leader, passionate about program, outspoken
Jack		African American	Learner, enthusiastic
Nicole	73	African American	Learner, reserved
Tina		African American	Learner, enthusiastic, optimistic, grateful for food produced from garden
Bonnie	54	African American	Learner, optimistic
Eric	30	African American	Learner, optimistic, thankful for program
Denise	19	African American	Observer, enthusiastic
Ann	19	African American	Leader, passionate, outspoken
Karen		African American	Learner, reserved
Monica	14	African American	Learner/leader, outspoken, optimistic, enthusiastic
Kerri		African American	Learner, reserved

In the adult focus group, four African American women and one African American male ages 54–73 participated. Like the young adult focus group, attendance dates of focus group participants averaged 3-days. Three of the adults already had gardens on their own. Please see Table One for brief demographic information about young adults and adults that participated in the focus groups. Also, note that all participant names were replaced with pseudonyms.

Data collection and analysis

The focus group took place at the community center that was on-site at the public housing complex. Data were collected through focus groups and observations. Attendance sheets were used to record attendance while observations conducted by a student intern recorded interactions among participants. The observations were expanded to create the Community Garden Education Program summary included in the previous section. Pre and post-surveys were also collected as part of Community Garden Education Program, but were not included in this analysis.

Prior to the focus group, Institutional Review Board approval was given for the focus groups. Participants gave informed consent and completed a short demographic and a post-survey before participating in the focus group.

During the focus groups, participants were asked about their experiences with the Community Garden Education Program. The interview guide consisted of open-ended questions and was developed for the focus group conversations. The questions were asked, but the focus group facilitator encouraged conversations relevant to the Community Garden Education Program to flow naturally. During our focus groups, the co-facilitator created a seating chart for participants and took notes during the sessions. All information from participants was audio-taped and transcribed in exact words by the co-facilitator. The co-facilitator used the seating chart to help identify who made each statement, which assured accuracy of recorded data. A debriefing session was held immediately after the focus groups, which included the facilitator and co-facilitator. Notes were made about initial impressions and expanded later the same day.

Data analysis consisted of coding and organizing information from observations, notes and transcriptions into themes. The constant comparative method was used as described by Glaser and Strauss (1967); data were coded and organized themes into general categories. Microanalysis or line by line analysis by reading through all transcripts and notes was first employed. Next, data from each line of transcripts and notes were then used with the comment tool in Microsoft Word to identify emerging themes within the text. The themes identified throughout the text formed initial categories. Each category was then identified by comment boxes; next each category was revised as more information was gathered and concepts emerged. As the concepts sharpened, each group of concepts was sorted into a separate Word document. For example, all data about learning was compiled together. This enabled exploration into contradictory cases and allowed adjustment of concepts accordingly. Next, links were explored among the concepts through theoretical comparisons relating to wellness and community development.

Theoretical comparison of concepts led to the hypothesis that these concepts could be grouped into issues relating to personal and relational wellness. We then compared the concepts from this research to the characteristics of individual and relational wellness that are part of the community wellness model. This comparison led to the results described in this article and to the conceptualization that community gardens can be used to promote collective wellness.

The trustworthiness of the data was increased in this research by including member checks. The findings from the focus groups were presented at a public housing complex to residents, WHA officials, facilitators, university students and faculty in a power point presentation that included time for questions. Those in attendance provided feedback and agreed with findings presented from the focus groups. Trustworthiness was also increased by audio-taping focus groups. Low inference description was obtained from transcripts

(LeCompte & Preissle, 1993) by transcribing data verbatim; exact words, phrases, pauses, and sounds were recorded to be included in data analysis.

Results

Personal Wellness

In community psychology, personal wellness includes intrapersonal factors like physical health, love, competence, and self-esteem. In health education/promotion, the sub-dimensions of personal wellness include physical, social, intellectual, emotional (mental), and spiritual issues. In this project, the concept of learning associated with the sub-dimension of intellectual personal wellness was important to both the young adults and adults groups. The young adults discussed the learning that occurred throughout the project. When asked for one word that described their role in the project, four of the participants said "Learner" and one participant named Brandy said "Doer."

Another result of the Community Garden Education Program was learning about gardening. One of the female adults, Brandy, said, "I learned how to do a soil sample. Something I never had a chance or opportunity to do." She also said "everybody got a chance to ask questions about what they was curious about and they got the answers." Another adult, Bonnie, commented:

> Because there's a lot of residents out here that want to participate but don't know how to get started. The children even want to know, and by everybody saying, well, this is an opportunity for everybody to have a chance to learn something.

The young adults also shared enthusiasm about learning about gardening. One of the female participants, Ann, explained:

> create a garden that we really wanted, that we really like was into. Like, just, it wasn't just to just to do it for fun. You really had to get into it and learn the process and learn the steps and learn what and what not to do.

Another participant, Monica, observed, "The successful part to me was the classes because…during the classes you got to actually ask what you, like, ask questions and get answers or whatever, so whenever you do the garden you know, like, what to do." While learning was important, it was a precursor to skill development resulting in a change in self-perception of participants, like Ann, who exclaimed excitedly, "We actually can say that we were gardeners!"

There were also immediate and tangible results from the Community Garden Education Program associated with personal physical health. The results identified by the focus group participants were eating more fruit and being able to provide food for themselves and their families. The young adults in particular pointed out that participating in the Community Garden Education Program increased their fruit consumption. Ann shared, "I've been eating fruit a lot. I've been telling my grandma to buy fruit." Another young participant, Denise, also added, "Well, like she said I have been eating a lot of fruits and stuff."

Another indicator of personal wellness was a sense of pride. Participants also discussed providing food for themselves and their families. Quotes from adults illustrated the pride associated with self-sustainability. Brandy, said with pride, "we got the most, best food, I mean the healthiest food in the United States." Another participant Tina said "I tell you one thing – what it means to me is we won't have to buy a whole lot of vegetables." Another participant added, "We can grow our own and we have enough to put in our freezer and things that lasts us." The project provided participants with vegetables that were unaffordable in the stores. Tina said:

But, um, the other people that grew cucumbers in their yard, I mean, they had cucumbers, and we was begging for 'em 'cause them things are expensive in the store ..I really appreciate what I got out of my garden. My little freezer's full.

This quote illustrates the how participants' access to vegetables was immediately affected by their participation in the Community Garden Education Program. Personal wellness was a primary theme in the data, but also associated with relational wellness that was achieved through the program.

Relational Wellness

Indicators of relational wellness include interpersonal factors like social support, affection, belonging, collaboration, respect for diversity, and democratic participation. According to the young adults, "it's basically about a group of people coming together, learning how to do one thing all together" and "you can learn from each other. You can learn from the old people, and the old people, they can learn from us."

Relational wellness was important to participants as illustrated through emphasis on community. The importance of community is illustrated in a quote from Ann, "I think that the most successful thing that we did was joining as a group to do other things." The following quote elaborates on the concept of community involvement:

> I think if we have one out here and they see people that's already out here that's involved maybe more will want to get involved because…you're not doing it for them, you're doing it for our community and the community, the whole community, needs to get involved in it.

One of the adults, Bonnie, also commented "And maybe too, if other people in the community are not involved, they see that we're committed to doing it, so they'll join and we can get more people and children involved."

Brandy, the self-identified "leader" of participants made the analogy that growing plants was like growing children: "Plants are similar to children or babies…. Because it starts from a seed and it takes care and loving and you can't give any baby any kind of food either because it'll spit it at you, right?" Furthermore, with agreement from other adult participants she said,"you got to mend your soil or whatever, it's the same thing as caring for a child."

Another theme regarding community focused on respect. Gaining and maintaining the respect of the community seemed to be a strategy identified by participants as a method of protecting their work. Bonnie reasoned:

> And then that way, when like children get involved, and the grown-ups, when stuff starts growing, you ain't got to worry about other children coming and trying to damage it 'cause the ones that's helping us will say "Oh, no, you can't go over there 'cause that's our work there.

Ann expressed her worry about a lack of respect:

> I'm really, I'm thinking, like, 'cause you know how when you start out your little gardens and stuff, like, you have some people out there that don't really care about that kind of stuff and just like throw trash or whatever in it. So, I'm kind of worried about that. Like, if we do start this up and it comes to be very successful, like, you have people out there that just don't think like we do.

The theme of worrying about protecting their work and gaining respect continued with "So they'll probably do something, like, they'll see a nice garden right there and they'll say

"Why don't we just tear it up," so I'm kind of worried about that."

Another theme was that in communities the gardens reflect the characters of the people who live there. An adult participant said, "I think yards tell a person what type of character – the person you are." Brandy further elaborates:

> No flowers. I mean, just shrubs…but if you gonna have a beautiful home and if you feel like you're the person that you're reflecting to people, why not let it come and greet the people as they come in?....if I had a car that breaks down in this neighborhood, I would be scared to go to the door. "Why, they're rich people?" and I said they don't have a character to their doorway.

As stated by the focus group participants, there is a sense of relational wellness that is apparent throughout the text.

Discussion

Literature reviews of community garden research reveal that personal wellness may be affected by participation in gardening. Austin, Johnston, and Morgan (2006) found that a community garden program for seniors had a significant affect on participants regarding social and emotional health. Milligan, Gatrell, and Bingley (2004) noted gardening activities led to a sense of achievement, satisfaction, and aesthetic pleasure for older people. The participants in this research emphasized that discussion of learning and skill building contributed to intellectual aspects of their personal wellness. Twiss et al (2003) cites community gardening efforts as contributing to knowledge and skill enhancement in participants.

Nutrition was another component of personal wellness discussed by participants. The young adults in particular pointed out that participating in the Community Garden Education Program increased their fruit consumption but did not mention vegetables as much as adults that participated in focus groups. Lineberger and Zajicek (2000) found after third and fifth grade children participated in a garden program designed to teach children about nutrition children liked vegetables more after participating in the program. However, preference for fruit scores did not improve significantly. Lautenschlager and Smith (2007) assert the inclusion of inner-city children and youth in community garden activities is essential to nutritional education to form healthy habits and lifestyle choices that will transfer into adulthood. Preliminary studies suggest that those who grow their own food have a higher intake of fruits and vegetables (Carter & Mann, 2006). Another study reported that community gardeners have greater consumption of fresh vegetables compared with non-gardeners, and lower consumption of sweet foods and drinks (Armstrong, 2000).

Relational Wellness

Research has shown that community gardens foster a sense of community (Shinew, Glover, & Parry, 2004). Armstrong (2000) stated that community gardens seemed to improve social networks and organizational capacity in low income and minority neighborhoods similar to the one in this study. Like in this research, Armstrong (2000) noted that community gardens created pride and attention to aesthetics in the neighborhood. However, relational wellness can also be affected negatively through community gardens. Schmelzkopf (1995) found conflicting advice, negotiating for gardening materials, and competition among non-profit groups created tension in a community garden effort.

In this research, relational wellness seemed to be improved through the sharing of fresh produce with neighbors. By sharing what was grown with neighbors, participants not only improved personal wellness but relational wellness as well. Focus group participants stressed their pride in being able to provide nutritious food for themselves and their families. Participants indicated they were able to save money on otherwise expensive foods. In addition, access to food from community gardens removed barriers such as transportation to grocery stores that were not located near the public housing complex.

Improving personal and relational wellness

Focus group data also disclosed information about how to improve learning and skill building activities. Twiss et al (2003) identified that leadership development is enhanced through experiential education including intergenerational and peer-to-peer learning. In opposition, research by Predny and Relf (2000) disclosed that intergenerational groups appeared to detract from personal participation in gardening activities. The young adults made it clear that instructional activities needed to be fun and as hands on as possible. In the Community Garden Education Program, it was evident that both the adults and the young adults responded better to instructors that were of the same generation. As a result, it would advisable to have both intergenerational and peer (same age group) instructors for both nutrition and gardening classes. The younger and older adults could be brought together to work on the garden after they have developed knowledge about the topics.

Another approach to improving personal wellness is to use best practice results to develop community garden course curriculums. Lautenschlager and Smith (2007) suggest that for youth a better understanding of the food system and learning to create their own food sources may improve food choices to optimize their health outcomes. In addition, community garden program curriculums could provide information about physical health benefits of gardening and encourage participants to work in the garden as way of improving physical health and function.

Approaches to promoting relational wellness include communal responsibility and the development of relationships within the larger community. Successful community garden projects can create opportunities for participants to take communal responsibility for the care and use of tools and common areas (Macias, 2008). Such projects also provide opportunities for relationships to form within the larger community. For example, focus group participants said they needed volunteers to help with heavy lifting and running machinery like tillers. The larger community where the Community Garden Education Program was conducted includes a community college and four-year university. Therefore, a tremendous opportunity for the development of internships or service learning opportunities exists within the community.

Collective Wellness

The concept of community wellness as proposed by Totikidis and Prilleltensky (2006) also includes collective wellness. For this article, we will examine food sustainability as a strategy for building collective wellness. Assistance with community organization seemed to be an area where focus group participants needed help.

Prilleltensky and Fox (2007) include equality, freedom, environment, and sustainability as indicators of collective wellness. In a discussion of public health implications of urban agriculture, Brown and Jameton (2000) discuss similar fundamental principles as ideals of collective wellness. They suggest the need to create a more equable society through the redistribution of income, education and employment, setting strict environmental regulations, alleviating hunger and preserving green space. Glover, Perry, and Shinew (2005) found in a community garden context "leisure episodes" were important to building social ties that contribute to the development of social capital, an element of collective wellness. Kingsley and Townsend (2006) also found membership in community garden efforts increased social capital. As noted in the relational wellness discussion, collective wellness as achieved through social capital community gardens may be positive or negative. Glover (2004) found social capital could be beneficial and costly depending on a participant's social position within the social network.

The aforementioned principles of social capital and sustainability can be addressed through the concept of community food security (CFS), which expands on food security by incorporating issues of human economics and social rights, community empowerment and self-reliance and a systematic understanding of natural food resources (Hamm & Bellows, 2003). According to the USDA, food security means that people have access, at all times, to enough food for an active, healthy life. The concept of CFS goes beyond the idea of food security by encompassing issues of collective wellness.

CFS as explained by Hamm & Bellows (2003) focuses on low income populations' needs for affordable, nutritionally-adequate food. In addition, food security needs to be defined in broad terms including social issues and policies. To obtain CFS, self-reliance/empowerment must be emphasized through enriching individuals' abilities to provide for their food needs like in community garden projects. CFS projects typically are "inter-disciplinary," crossing many boundaries and incorporating collaborations with multiple agencies.

Focus group participants expressed enthusiasm for continuing the community garden project and making it their own neighborhood garden within the housing development. The foundations of CFS and collective wellness were apparent as participants gladly took on the responsibility of recruiting more community members to become involved in the project.

In order to achieve CFS, and ultimately collective wellness, increased funding and comprehensive policy are needed. Participants not only wanted to continue the project, but to expand it as well. Additional public and private funds could ensure sustainability of this community garden as stated by Brown & Jameton (2000), "Public and private funding for initiatives like the USDA Food Security program can create the opportunity for even more comprehensive responses that link low-income consumers and local produce growers" (p. 27). Collective wellness could be achieved by meeting the needs of low-income people by increasing community self-reliance through access to fresher, more nutritious food supplies.

In order to achieve CFS, Bellows and Hamm (2003) suggest the development of community coalitions for two reasons: 1) the coalition helps establish a conceptual framework that represents all the stakeholders involved and can provide lobbying and 2) the framework assists organizations and individuals understand their role in larger social change efforts. Here are specific suggestions for this community garden project that may help establish CFS and contribute to collective wellness: 1) engage community organizations through commitment of local leadership 2) Provide skill-building opportunities for participants, and 3) provide land for gardens on-site in public housing developments.

Commitment of community organizations through development of local leadership is an integral component of community gardens. While many residents of disadvantaged communities may desire a community garden, they may not have the resources or know who to contact to create a gardening program. Brown and Jameton (2000) suggest that attending a community meeting on a garden project can introduce residents to non-profit and government officials they might never have known about and vice versa. One way to connect residents with community resources is through the creation of a Community Garden Coalition. Such a coalition would create the opportunity to get more people from the community involved. The Community Garden Coalition should include residents of the community, representatives from the local housing authority, schools and churches. The Community Garden Coalition could also include representatives from the American Community Garden Association, the local USDA Cooperative Extension Service, local farms or nurseries, and /or local

University. Ultimately, a Community Garden Coalition would help with policy and advocacy issues that contribute to CFS and collective wellness.

Another important component of building CFS toward collective wellness is skill-building. When planning community gardens, we believe it is important to provide educational opportunities like the Community Garden Education Program that help build skills of participants. In addition to learning about gardening and nutrition, we believe residents would benefit from classes on community engagement and organization. Such educational opportunities would benefit individuals and the community garden while "planting the seed" for social change in the community.

In addition to the development of a Community Garden Coalition and skill-building of participants, we recommend that land be provided for a community garden at each public housing site. Specifically for the Community Garden Education Program, more land on-site would be beneficial and more convenient then an off-site plot. In order to start a community garden for public housing or any other site, work with a Community Garden Coalition to develop a plan, budget, recruit volunteers, and solicit donations for needed resources. It is important to seek various funding opportunities as community gardens may qualify for both private and public grants. In addition, check local farming ordinances and possible needs for liability insurance.

There are many free resources available online to guide the process of starting a community garden. The American Community Garden Association (2008) provides a step-by-step summary of how to start a community garden. Some of the most salient steps include: choosing a site that gets at least 6 hours of sunshine a day, that is located near a water source, and has proper drainage. Also, conducting a soil test in the fall to assess nutrients, heavy metals and any potential contaminates is necessary. In order to prepare and develop a site, clean the location, plan the garden layout including a storage area for tools, other equipment, and allowing for a compost area; decide if the garden will be organic; create a volunteer work schedule. In order to prevent vandalism, promote ownership and pride in the community that may help build CFS, use signs and bulletin boards to promote the garden as a neighborhood project.

Summary

Community gardens can be much more than a plot of land. A well planned and coordinated community garden has the potential to help improve the personal and relational wellness of participants while promoting community food security that may led to collective wellness. We believe successful and sustainable community gardening programs can only occur through the cooperation and commitment of residents, community leaders and local government. While educational programs need to include information on nutrition and gardening, we also believe it is important to educate participants about community building and engagement. In total, community gardens not only improve the quality of life of individuals, but can help improve the collective wellness of an entire community.

References

American Community Garden Association (2008). *Starting a community garden*. Retrieved on December 14, 2008 from http://www.communitygarden.org/learn/starting-a-community-garden.php#choose

Armstrong, D. (2000). A survey of community gardens in upstate New York: Implications for health promotion and community development. *Health & Place, 6*, 319 – 327.

Austin, E.N., Johnston, Y.A.M & Morgan, L.L. (2006). Community gardening in a senior center: A therapeutic intervention to improve the health of older adults. *Therapeutic Recreation Journal, 40* (1), 48-56.

Bellows, A.C. & Hamm, M.W. (2003). International effects on and inspiration for community food security policies and practices in the USA. *Critical Public Health, 13* (2), 107-123.

Brown, K.H. & Jameton, A.L. (2000). Public health implications of urban agriculture. *Journal of*

Public Health Policy, 21, 20 – 39.

Cadell, S., Karabanow, J. & Sanchez, M. (2001). Community, empowerment, and resilience: Path to wellness. *Canadian Journal of Community Mental Health, 20* (1), 21-35.

Carter, A. & Mann, P. (2006). Farming from the city center to the urban fringe: Urban planning and food security. Fact sheet prepared for North American Urban Agriculture Committee of the Food Security Coalition.

Corbin, C.B. & Pangrazi, R.P. (2001). Toward a uniform definition of wellness: A commentary. *President's Council on Physical Fitness and Sports Research Digest, 3,* 1-8.

Evans, S.D. & Prilleltensky, I. (2007). Youth and democracy: Participation for personal, relational, and collective well-being. *Journal of Community Psychology, 35* (6), 681-692.

Glover, T.D., Parry, D.C. & Shinew, K.J. (2005). Building relationships, accessing resources: Mobilizing social capital in community garden contexts. *Journal of Leisure Research, 37* (4), 450-474.

Glover, T.D., Shinew, K.J. & Parry, D.C. (2005). Association, sociability, and civic culture: The demographic effect of community gardening. *Leisure Sciences, 27,* 75-92.

Hamm, M.W. & Bellows, A.C. (2003). Community of food security and nutrition educators. *Journal of Nutrition Education Behavior, 35,* 37-43.

Hanna, A. K. & Oh, P. (2000). Rethinking urban poverty: A look at community gardens. *Bulletin of Science, Technology & Society, 20 (3),* 207-216.

Kingsley, J. & Townsend, M. (2006). 'Dig In' to social capital: Community gardens as mechanisms for growing urban social connectedness. *Urban Policy and Research, 24* (4), 525-537.

Lautenschlager, L. and Smith, C. (2007). Beliefs, knowledge, and values held by inner-city youth about gardening, nutrition, and cooking. *Agriculture and Human Values, 24:* 245-258.

LeCompte, M.D. & Preissle, J. (1993). *Ethnography and qualitative design in education research.* New York: Academic Press.

Lineberger, S.E. & Zajicek, J.M. (2000). School gardens: Can a hands-on teaching tool affect students' attitudes and behaviors regarding fruit and vegetables? *HortTechnology, 10* (3), 593-597.

Macias, T. (2008). Working toward a just, equitable, and local food system: The social impact of community-based agriculture. *Social Science Quarterly, 89 (5):* 1086-1101.

Malakoff. D. (1995). What good is community greening? *ACGA Community Greening Review.16-20.*

Milligan, C., Gatrell, A., & Bingley, A. (2004). 'Cultivating health': Therapeutic landscapes and older people in Northern England. *Social Science & Medicine, 58,* 1781-1793.

Morsillo, J. & Prilleltensky, I. (2007). Social action with youth: Interventions, evaluation, and psychopolitical validity. *Journal of Community Psychology, 35* (6), 725-740.

Predney, M.L.& Relf, D. (2000). Interactions between elderly adults and preschool children in horticultural therapy research program. *HortTechnology, 10* (1), 64-70.

Prilleltensky, I. (2005). Promoting well-being: Time for a paradigm shift in health and human services. *Scandinavian Journal of Public Health, 33,* 53-60.

Prilleltensky, I. & Fox, D.R. (2007). Psychopolitical literacy for wellness and justice. *Journal of Community Psychology, 35* (6), 793-805.

Prilleltensky, I. & Nelson, G. (2000). Promoting child and family wellness: Priorities for psychological and social interventions. *Journal of Community and Applied Social Psychology, 10,* 85-105.

North Carolina State Center for Health Statistics. (2006). *2005 BRFSS Survey Results: New Hanover County.* Retrieved on January 4, 2009 http://www.schs.state.nc.us/SCHS/brfss/2005/nc/afam/rf1.html

Schmelzkopf, K. (1995). Urban community gardens as a contested space. *Geographical Review, 85* (3), 364-380.

Schukoske, J. E. (2000). Community development through gardening: State and local policies transforming urban open space. *Legislation & Public Policy, 3,* 351-392.

Shinew, K.J., Glover, T.D. & Parry, D.C. (2004). Leisure spaces as potential sites for interracial interaction: Community gardens in urban areas. *Journal of Leisure Research, 36* (3), 336-355.

Totikidis, V. & Prilleltensky, I. (2006). Engaging community in cycle of praxis: Multicultural perspectives on personal, relational and collective wellness. *Community, work and family, 9* (1), 48-66.

Twiss, J., Dickinson, J., Duma, S., Kleinman, T., Paulsen, H., & Rilveria, L. (2003). Community gardens: Lessons learned from California healthy cities and communities. *American Journal of Public Health, 93,* 1435 – 1438.

Index

References to Tables and Figures are in **bold** type

agritourism 55
agroecosystems 10
A Kingdom So Delicious 56
Alabama Farmers markets 64–81; excerpt of questionnaire tool **81**; future research 78; general demographic information of visitors **71**; intrinsic value 76; questionnaire 70; reasons for visits to 76; research methods 69–71; research results 71–6; selected differences between two groups of visitors **72**
Alonso, Abel 6
alternative food networks 37
Ann Arbor, Michigan 25
asset-based approach 36, 39
Auburn University 69

breweries 55
bridging networks 43
business clusters 22–34; qualitative determination 24–5; triangulation appproach 24
buy local approach 9
buy local campaigns 19–20

capital: types 37
Carden, Andrea 6
Catfish Institute 29
Community food security (CFS) 91–2
City of Valley 69
civicness 43
cluster identification 24
collective wellness 90–2
community 10
community capital 35–52; alternative sources 41; analytical strategy 44; background variables 43; bivariate correlations 44–5; conventional sources 41; data 40; descriptive statistics 44–5; food sources, and 48; independent variables 41–3; mail survey 40; measurement 41; methods 40; research limitations 49; sample 40; search terms 41

community development 2–3, 36
community economy 16
Community Garden Education Program 82–93; data collection and analysis 86–7; participants 85; research methodology 84–6
community gardens 4
community organizations: commitment 91–2
community wellness 82–93
consumers 1
conventional versus alternative food networks 36
cost differential 5
Crowe, Jessica 5
Community support agriculture (CSA) 4
CSAs: statistics 26
culinary tourism 53–63; cost disconnect 61; implications 61; linkages 61; research methods 48–9; statistics 54; wide variety 62
cultural capital 38; embodied 39; legacy 38; measurement 41–3

D'Abundo, Michelle 6
Door County Economic Development Corporation (DCEDC) 56
defensive localism 69
Delta catfish farms 29
direct sales 60
Door County, Wisconsin 55
Dougherty, Michael L 5

economic drivers 43–4
economic factors 49
economic gardening 23
economic hunting 23
education 48
entrepreneurial social infrastructure (ESI) 37–8
export orientated clusters 23
export orientated/local cluster divide 25

farmers markets 64–81; historical development 67; meaning 67; multiple

INDEX

beneficial effects 66–9; quality of produce 30; social fabric, and 67–8; statistics 55
farmer's perspective 18
farm-to-school programs 3–4
fish boil 56
food clusters 22–34
food insecurity 35–52; personal risk factors 39
food options 35–52
foodsheds 10
food sources: community capital, and 48
free trade agreements 18

Harvard Business School 25
helping local farmers 17
home 10
human capital 39–40; measurement 43
hunger 35
hybrid cluster 30
improving personal and relational wellness 90
institutions: local foods, and 54
interpretations of local **14**

gardening 82–93
global food system: criticism of 1
globalization 66
going back to basics 77
grass-root consumer groups 77
Green, Gary 5

local: contracting ways of conceptualising **13**; meaning 9–10; qualitative attributes 15; ranking among other consumer values and interests 17; relational attributes 15; spatial perceptions 19
local business clusters 22–34
local clusters: examples 24; existence proof 31; indirect benefits 31
local economic activity 22
local economy 16
local food 8–21; advantages 54; data sets 11; demand 55, 57; direct sales 60; everyday meanings 8–21; percent consumers rating "very important" 17; pinning down the local 12–13; retailer reasons for not purchasing additional items **60**; retailer reasons for choosing to source **58**; retailer reasons for deciding to increase amount 59; study methods 11–19; supply of 57; telephone survey 11
local food movement 1
local food systems: contributions of 2
local market 14; spatial defintion 16
local markets; importance for Washington farmers 18–19; producers' motivations for supplying 60
local sector activity 25
locally grown 17

locavores 2
locally-oriented import substitution (LOIS) 23

Maine: agricultural production 27; potatoes 28
Maine Local Produce cluster (MELP) 26–8; local cluster, as 27; strong economic growth 29
Miller, Chad 5
Minnesota: trail system 53
Mississippi catfish cluster (MSC) 28–9; associated institutions 29
Missouri Regional Cuisines Project 53
The Maine Organic Farmers and Gardeners Association (MOFGA) 27

New Hanover County 82
nuanced technology 24
nutrition 89

O'Neill, Martin 6
Obesity Prevention Initiative (OPI) 82
organic 17
Ostrom, Marcia 5

Peninsula Arts & Humanities Alliance (PAHA) 56
percentages and means for selected variables **42**
personal wellness 87–8
place 10
poisson regression 44, 45–8

regional economy 54
relational wellness 88–9
restaurant market 61

Smith, Justin 5
Supplemental Nutrition Assistance Program (SNAP) 5
social capital 37–8
social fabric: investing in 64–81
spatial constructions of scale 13
supply and demand 4
supply chain 3
sustainable agriculture 27

Taylor, Davis 5

USDA statistics 26

values-based commitments 3
Variance Inflation Factor 44
varieties of local food systems 3–4
Vietnam 29

wellness 82–93
wine industry 55
world catfish festival 29